Rhodes

Rhodes

Original text by Lindsay Bennett
Updated by Paul Hellander
Photography: Pete Bennett
Cover photograph by Pete Bennett
Photo Editor: Naomi Zinn
Layout: Media Content Marketing, Inc.
Cartography by Raffaele De Gennaro
Managing Editor: Clare Peel
Series Editor: Tony Halliday

Fifth Edition 2002. Updated 2004

CONTACTING THE EDITORS
Every effort has been made to provide accurate information in this publication, but changes are inevitable. The publisher cannot be responsible for any resulting loss, inconvenience or injury. We would appreciate it if readers would call our attention to any errors or outdated information by contacting Berlitz Publishing, PO Box 7910, London SE1 1WE, England. Fax: (44) 20 7403 0290; e-mail: berlitz@apaguide.co.uk; www.berlitzpublishing.com

CONTENTS

● A  in the text denotes a highly recommended sight

Rhodes

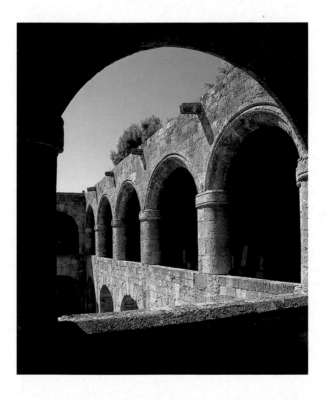

THE ISLAND AND
ITS PEOPLE

It's impossible not to feel the weight of history when you arrive in Rhodes. The granite of Mycenaean settlements, marble of Classical sites and stone of medieval churches and castles are all tangible legacies of the long historical timeline. It is even said that Greek Gods were born on Rhodes; indeed, the island itself was a gift from Helios, the sun god, to his favourite nymph Rhodon.

However, to believe that Rhodes is simply an island for archaeology buffs stuck in the past would be erroneous. With long hot summer days, warm waters, numerous beaches and lots to do, it is a fun-lovers' paradise in summer.

Rhodes is the largest island in the Dodecanese, a group that lies in the southeastern Aegean Sea between Greece and Turkey. Originally twelve islands (dódeka nisiá means 'twelve islands' in Greek) that formed an alliance against Turkish repression in the early part of the 20th century, the group is now an administrative region of over 200 islands, though only a handful have a viable population. Today very much part of Greece, the Dodecanese group was a late addition to the Greek state – they were only joined with their spiritual homeland in 1947.

The ebb and flow of history has certainly washed over Rhodes. Periods of influence and great wealth have been interspersed with centuries as a backwater, with each period leaving its mark in the sands of time.

A triumvirate of city states developed in the second and first millennia BC when Rhodes rivalled cities such as Athens and Corinth in terms of importance. The population was adept at commerce and cultivated trading partners around the Mediterranean, bringing sustained prosperity to its people.

Later there was status with a famed School of Oratory, and the magnificent statue — the Colossus — a 'wonder' of the ancient world. Lying only 20 km (12 miles) from the Turkish coastline Rhodes was a stepping stone on the long trade routes between east and west throughout Classical Greek, Hellenistic and Roman times, benefitting from port taxes that swelled its coffers.

Throughout most of the last two millennia, this strategically important territory was fought over by European superpowers, and its people became deeply embroiled in the religious conflicts between Christianity and Islam. As the Roman Empire disintegrated, Rhodes became an undefended outpost of Byzantium, nominally ruled from Constantinople but left to the mercy of marauding pirates. Its population lived in fear until the 14th century, when it became home to the Order of the Knights of St John, newly ousted from the Holy Land by Muslim forces.

When these soldiers of Christ arrived on the island they changed the landscape irrevocably, undertaking a huge building programme that created the strongest fortifications in Europe. The citadel that is Rhodes Old Town still stands as a monument to their wealth, steadfastness and faith; strong thick walls encircle medieval buildings so unique that it has been designated a World Heritage site. However, it was not invincible in its heyday. During the 16th century Ottoman Turkish forces drove the knights east and took up residence, creating a comfortable western outpost of their eastern civilisation. The Turks aroused an animosity that persisted long after their departure in the early years of the 20th century, yet their influence can be seen in elegant minarets, carved marble fountains and delicate wooden balconied windows in the Old Town.

Italy ousted the Turks just before World War I and settled in to turn their temporary jurisdiction into a permanent residency. They invested vast sums of money, improving the infrastructure and for the first time the ancient sites were subjected to serious archaeological study.

Despite these numerous landlords, the basic elements of the way of life of ordinary people of Rhodes changed little for over 5,000 years. The seas produced abundant food for the earliest settlers; the warm summers brought forth crops of grain and have provided grazing for herds of goats since the fifth century BC. In the Bronze Age, donkeys and mules provided a means of transport, and at around the same time the first

A vendor cleans up – natural sponges for sale in Rhodes Old Town.

olive trees and vines bore fruits. Life was governed by seasons of planting, tending and harvesting.

From the early Christian era the fabric of life has been sustained by religion. The church (particularly the Orthodox religion) was identified with all that was Greek long before the modern state was created in 1832. Throughout natural disaster, war, disease and occupation, the church has been there as a place of refuge and solace, both physically and spiritually. Women have traditionally formed the majority of the congregation, praying for protection for their fathers, husbands and sons that were diving for sponges or away at sea in merchant fleets. All across the island small, whitewashed, churches house a simple cross, icon and lit candles; a number also have incredible frescoes adorning their domes and walls.

Yet island life has seen more change in the last 20 years than perhaps it had in the previous thousand. Rhodes is now 'invaded' by over one million people each year creating both fantastic opportunities and great pressures for the island and its people. Over half of the island population now lives in Rhodes Town and takes advantage of the many commercial opportunities.

The major resorts are international territories, with restaurant signs and menus in English along with daily English-language newspapers, imported beer and sports bars with satellite broadcasts. As most hotel and tourism workers speak English, you

Rhodes Old Town is a quaint village, but it has a thriving community that welcomes visitors from around the world.

may not even realise that you are in Greece – if you choose not to venture out from the resort to explore the island.

Tourism has brought wealth and security, and the current generation expects more than the simple lives experienced by their parents and grandparents. As incomes have risen, farmers have bought trucks to replace their trusty donkeys; many farmers are likely to give up their trade altogether to open a bar or car-rental office. You'll find that some fishermen now use their boats to ferry tourists to nearby beaches rather than to catch fish. Mobile phones are heard far more frequently than the haunting cadences of the *bouzouki*, and only the old-timers have time to linger over a game of backgammon at the *kafenion* while the younger men strive to impress the girls with their new fast cars. There's a sophistication here not found in many towns in the Aegean – a casino, modern boutiques selling all the latest designer streetwear, and teenage girls going out for the night without the chaperone that was considered an absolute necessity only a generation ago.

However, though Rhodes has given up many of its traditional ways, some things haven't changed. The family is still at the heart of life and each new addition is proudly shown off at the evening stroll *(volta)*. Children play happily and safely in the streets, watched over by doting grandparents. A Greek gathering of family and friends would not be complete without ardent debate. After all, this was the country that invented democratic decision-making through discussion; and if the conversation gets a little noisy then all the better, the sound of the Greek language seems to be made for animated argument – and it seems that no-one ever goes home bearing a grudge.

Rhodians see visitors as *xenos* (the word means both stranger and foreigner), and their hospitality is genuine and

Local fisherman earnestly bring forth the bounty of the Aegean Sea.

refreshing. A pocketful of Greek phases used at the *taverna* will earn you honest appreciation and produce smiles and approving nods from the older gentlemen enjoying a leisurely lunch or dinner.

Rural life can still be found despite the growth of the resorts, especially as you travel south. Here, goatherds and their flocks still rest under the shade of a plane tree, and grapes ripen slowly on low-growing vines with the rays of the summer sun.

Rhodes has grasped the opportunity of catering to the modern era for worshippers of the sun-god Helios with both hands, and it provides an excellent product for its visitors. Good transport connections, a plethora of eateries, bars and nightclubs and a relaxed welcoming attitude all contribute to a great holiday experience. Spring or autumn are ideal times for walking and hiking, and in summer you can simply take in the sun or enjoy a range of watersports, the latest hair-raising amusement ride and golf. Above all, let's not forget the enigmatic mixture of historical influences to explore here and the unique architecture of Rhodes Old Town. Whatever your interests there's bound to be something in Rhodes to suit you. Perhaps this is why so many people keep coming back for more.

HISTORY

I n ancient Greek mythology, Rhodes was the domain of the Helios, the sun god, and was known as Heliousa, the Sun-friend. Helios gave the island to his favourite, a nymph named Rhodon, and Rhodes was christened.

Few traces remain of the first human inhabitants. They were a primitive and rugged people from Asia Minor that could fashion simple tools, and cast pottery. From 2500–1500 BC, the Bronze Age, Carians from Anatolia and Phoenicians from Lebanon settled on the island and then moved west to Crete and beyond. Minoan merchants from Crete set up shop in the Rhodian ports of Líndos, Kámiros and Ialysós (named after the grandsons of Helios), as part of a lucrative trading network that included Egypt and the Levant. Each port was an independent city-state with its own economy and government.

The Making of a Nation

Some undetermined cataclysm wreaked havoc on the Minoan civilisation around 1450 BC. The remaining population was driven from Crete by invaders from the Greek mainland, the Achaeans, who also occupied Rhodes. These people were the Greeks of Homer's *Iliad*, seafaring warriors who had pushed south through Athens. When the Achaeans launched their famous 1,000 ships against Troy, according to Homer 'nine ships of the arrogant Rhodians' sailed with Agamemnon's fleet. The 10-year war ended with the destruction of Troy, but it also exhausted the conquerors. They were no match for the tall, blond and savage Dorians from the Balkans, who swept through Greece in 1200 BC. The fusion of the Dorians with the Aegean people eventually produced the Classical period of Greek civilisation.

The history of Greece is well represented at Rhodes' Archaeological Museum.

By 700 BC, Rhodian city-states, together with the Asia Minor ports of Halicarnassus (now Bodrum) and Knidos, and the island of Kos, had set up a six-city trading league under Dorian charter, the Hexapolis. Each city minted its own coins (money had just been invented in Asia Minor), and Líndos dispatched merchants with instructions to colonise parts of the western Mediterranean.

In the fifth century BC, a large force dispatched to conquer lands in the west by the king of Persia, Darius, reached the Aegean. The city-states of mainland Greece – Athens and Sparta – now stood in the way of its drive. Anticipating a Greek defeat, Rhodes joined forces with the Persians, but the tide turned at the land battle of Marathon in 490 BC. When the Greeks sank the fleet of Darius' son, Xerxes, at the epic sea battle of Salamis ten years later, there were around 40 Rhodian ships among the victims. The Greeks exacted swift retribution on the islands that had sided with the defeated enemy.

The Delian League was founded soon afterwards, under leadership from Athens, as an attempt to bring unity and security to the Greek city and island states, and Rhodes soon became a taxpaying member. This league did much to ensure economic and political strength for the region over the coming centuries.

The Founding of Rhodes Town

Due to its strategic position on vital trade routes in the eastern Mediterranean, Rhodes grew in importance as a maritime power and centre of finance. By 408 BC, the volume of trade and shipping had become too much for the island's three ports to handle, and, by mutual consent, the City of Rhodes was founded. Well-situated at the northern tip of the island with five large natural harbours, it was the perfect answer. The design of the wide streets was based on the grid pattern of the famous architect Hippodamus of Miletus, and many of today's thoroughfares still follow the same plan. The new city prospered, while Ialysós and Kámiros went into decline, eventually becoming little more than centres of religion.

When it became clear that Alexander the Great was worthy of the name, Rhodes sided with him and benefited from trade concessions with Egypt, the Macedonian's next conquest. After the great leader's death in 323 BC, Rhodes refused to join with an expedition by his successor, Antigonus, against Ptolemy I, the Macedonian general who had become the king of Egypt. This led to an attack on the city in 305 BC by Antigonus' son Demetrius, known as 'the Besieger'.

Demetrius had an army of 40,000 troops, but his *pièce de résistance* was the Helepolis, an ingenious siege machine that was nine storeys high. Made of huge amounts of heavy and expensive bronze it was propelled on wheels of oak and heaved right up to the ramparts of the fortified city by a crew of 3,400 people.

The siege machine was not successful in defeating the city, and hostilities ended in a truce. Demetrius then handed over the remains of his battle equipment to the Rhodians, asking them to sell it and build a commemorative monument of the siege from the proceeds. Thus was born the famous Colossus, one of the Seven Wonders of the Ancient World.

Alliance with Rome

At the peak of its power, and with a population about three times that of today, Rhodes enjoyed a golden age in the third century BC. The island won fame as a cultural and intellectual centre, with its renowned School of Rhetoric founded in 342 BC by the Athenian Aeschines. Rhodian artists and craftsmen, passing on skills from generation to generation, enjoyed a privileged social standing and were regarded highly throughout the Mediterranean. When the Colossus was toppled by an earthquake in 227 BC, the rest of the city was destroyed too, but such was its prestige in the Hellenistic world that sufficient financial and technical help was sent in to rebuild it.

In 166 BC, Rhodes refused to side with Rome in a disagreement over hostilities against Perseus of Macedonia. As a punishment, Rome took away one of the island's important protectorates: Delos. It declared the island a free port, thus depriving Rhodes of a substantial income from port duties. Rhodians took immediate note of the threat and, in 164 BC, concluded an alliance with Rome. However, this brought a new dilemma, which side to take in Rome's civil wars and internal struggles. Rhodes supported Pompeii versus Julius Caesar, but after his defeat of the Rhodians, Caesar forgave them and re-cemented the alliance. Then Cassius and Brutus, Caesar's assassins, demanded that Rhodes help in their war against the senate. When this was refused, Cassius besieged, conquered and sacked Rhodes. He plundered 3,000 statues and dispatched them to Rome, leaving nothing but *The Sun* – a famous sculpture by

Lysippus of the chariot of Helios, too heavy to remove. Almost all of this precious art was destroyed when Rome burned in AD 64.

In the Name of God

Christianity took root during the first century, aided by St Paul, who visited the island on his way to Syria, 20 years after the Crucifixion. However, the new religion did not bring stability for the island's population. The City of Rhodes was twice shattered by earthquakes – in AD 155 and again in 515. Much weakened, it became a prime target for armies of invaders – plundered by the Goths in AD 263, overrun by Persians and Arabs in the seventh century, and unceasingly harassed by pirates. Although nominally part of the Byzantine Empire, Rhodes was on its own as far as defense was concerned.

By the 11th century, followers of Muhammad had conquered Jerusalem, implanted their faith in Persia and North Africa, converted the Turks and occupied more than half of Spain's territory. To Christians, they represented an enormous threat to their faith and to the security of Europe.

Rhodes' ties with Western Europe were strengthened –

Icons from the Byzantine Empire represent the early stronghold of Christianity.

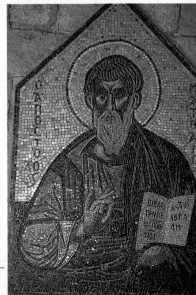

Hippocrates Square is the centre of a day's exploration around the Old Town.

first through the resumption of trade with Venice and then, in 1097, with the appearance of the first crusaders on their eastward journey to Jerusalem. In 1191, Richard the Lionheart of England and Philip Augustus of France landed in Rhodes to recruit mercenaries for another crusade. However, in the 13th century the tide of battle turned, and by 1291 the Christian army was forced off the beaches at Acre (now part of Israel), losing their last foothold in the Holy Land.

Among the retreating soldiers were the Knights of the Order of St John, founded in Jerusalem more than two centuries earlier to offer succour and medical help to pilgrims. During the Crusades these Knights Hospitalers became more and more militaristic. Forced to fight off repeated Muslim attacks, they had learned the value of fortified walls. When ordered to regroup, the Knights settled on Cyprus, but as the Muslim threat to that island began to grow, they moved to Rhodes, deciding that it would make a better bastion.

Since the fierce Genoese pirates that had taken Rhodes in 1248 would not let them settle there, the Knights decided to buy the island from them. The Byzantine emperor who laid nominal historic claim to the island was most displeased, but by 1309 the Knights had settled in and started the elaborate fortifications. Over the next 213 years they continued to improve the defenses, fighting off repeated Muslim assaults while also continuing to maintain a 'state-of-the-art' hospital.

Outside the city, the Knights extended their system of defenses with some 30 fortresses strung across the land and yet more on outlying islands. On both land and sea the Knights were formidable warriors, undaunted in their defense of the Cross. In 1444, aided by 5,000 Rhodian supporters, they resisted attack by the Sultan of Egypt. Thirty-six years later they brilliantly out-manoeuvred the forces of Muhammad II, the Conqueror.

Under the Ottomans

Turkish Ottoman power was growing in the eastern Mediterranean, and Rhodes was a prime target for them. In 1522 Suleiman the Magnificent moved against the Knights. On 24 June his massive force landed close to Ialysós. Shuttling back and forth from the Turkish mainland, 200 ships carried 150,000 soldiers, equipment, food and supplies to lay siege to Rhodes.

In four and a half months, Suleiman lost 50,000 men in attempting to take the fortified city. The Turks were on the verge of giving up when a traitor, Amaral, revealed that the Christians were also at the end of their tether. Suleiman decided to go all out and breach the walls. The Rhodians, facing famine, called for a truce.

And so, on 1 January 1523, after 145 days of siege, the 180 remaining Knights were allowed to leave honourably, eventually finding a new base on the island of Malta. They took with them 8,000 Christians, church banners and a variety of art treasures and relics.

For nearly four centuries, until 1912, Rhodes remained a minor Turkish possession. No mass development took place in Rhodes Town. The Grand Masters' Palace became a cattle barn, and once-noble inns were converted to barracks. Only Turks and Jews were allowed to live in the walled city; every night at the curfew bell, the Greeks working there had to leave for their homes in outlying villages. A new city, Néa Chóra (now Neochori), was established outside and around the city walls. This division of the two cultures did ensure that traditional Greek customs survived and even prospered, with firm links to other Greek populations through the Orthodox Church. In 1821 mainland Greece revolted against the Turks and eventually won independence. Rhodes, too, tried to throw off its yoke but failed, suffering brutally as the Turks quashed the revolt.

However, Ottoman fortunes were in decline by the end of the 19th century, and territory continued to trickle out of its control. Siding with Germany in World War I saw its final demise, but not before Italy scored the first victory with the Treaty of Lausanne in 1912. A clause gave them leave to take over the Dodecanese islands – ostensibly in trust for eventual union with Greece.

Helios Worship Returns

Unlike the Turks during their period of domination, the Italians immediately set to work excavating and restoring Classical and medieval sites, and constructing roads, homes and public buildings. They removed all Turkish appendages from buildings in the Knights' Quarter, and restored – to their own plans – the Palace of the Grand

Masters as a summer residence for Victor Emmanuel III and, later, Mussolini (the king was overthrown before he could ever use it). Much was destroyed in their zeal, and the Rhodians suffered hardship under the occupation. However, the Italians made the island far more accessible and were responsible for the beginning of its development as a tourist destination.

As time passed, it became increasingly clear that Italy had no intention of returning the Dodecanese islands to Greece, as had been the promise. In the late 1930s, the Greek language and Greek Orthodox Church were officially outlawed, with the intention of creating a greater Italian Empire in the eastern Mediterranean. World War II would have a terminal effect on this plan.

After Mussolini's government was defeated in 1943, German troops landed on Rhodes and took over all the Italian military bases. The islands were finally liberated by British forces and, after temporary United Nations trusteeship, were united with mainland Greece in 1947. Rhodes gained duty-free status, and Greece made plans to develop the tourist industry. Hotels were built and facilities expanded.

This bronze deer stands at the entrance to Rhodes' Mandráki Harbour.

Today, tourist facilities are still expanding, and Rhodes still succumbs to almost year-round foreign invasion. The cobbled streets of the Old Town are filled with the sounds of many tongues, but these invaders are generally welcome, bringing with them a certain prosperity and stability. They come simply to enjoy the island's architectural heritage – many sites are now considered so important that they have been declared UNESCO World Heritage sites – and to worship Helios, the sun.

A World Wonder

Contrary to popular belief, the Colossus of Rhodes did not straddle the entrance to Mandráki Harbour – its 20 tons of bronze would have sunk immediately into the seabed. Instead, more recent theories place the statue of Rhodes' protector, the sun god Helios, near the Palace of the Grand Masters.

Sculptor Chares of Líndos took 12 years to cast the Colossus, finishing his 30-m (105-ft) masterpiece around 290 BC. Each finger, we are told, was the size of a man. Despite the fact that his work was considered one of the Seven Wonders of the Ancient World, Chares committed suicide after discovering a mistake in his calculations. During an earthquake, less than 70 years after its completion, the Colossus cracked at the knees and crashed to the ground.

City fathers consulted the Oracle at Delphi who warned them not to restore the statue. The crumpled image lay where it had fallen for nearly 900 years until the mid-seventh century, when Arab pirates sacked Rhodes and sold off the bronze as scrap to a Jewish merchant from Syria who, legend says, needed 900 camels to carry it off.

WHERE TO GO

Rhodes is an easy island to explore, and its major settlements are car-free, meaning that you can stroll around at your own leisure. With a good road network and public transport for those who want to take an independent route, or numerous professional tour companies for those who want an organised itinerary, it helps the visitor to get the best out of its attractions.

This guide is divided into four sections, exploring Rhodes Old and New Town first before heading off down the western side of the island. Then tour the eastern coast, with a separate section on the ancient town of Líndos halfway down the coast.

RHODES TOWN

The Old Town

Nothing quite prepares you for the spectacle that is Rhodes Old Town. An immense citadel with high sandstone walls 4 km (2.5 miles) long, set by the town's five natural harbours, it immediately takes you back in time. Built on the site of ancient Rhodes, begun some four centuries prior to the birth of Christ, the Old Town came to serve as the headquarters of the Knights of St John in 1309, one of the most powerful organisations of the early second millennium. Their principle aim was to provide medical care for pilgrims on their journeys to the Holy Land, but they became one of the leading military opponents of Islam and the front line against the fierce Muslim armies coming from the East. In 1522, after a long siege, Ottoman forces wrenched Rhodes from the grasp of the Knights and thus began four hundred years of Muslim Turkish rule. Vestiges of their influence can still be found within the walls. The turn of the 20th century saw the Ottomans in decline and in 1912, following the Italian-Turkish War, the Dodecanese islands (including Rhodes), were ceded to Italy. A great deal of time and money was invested in renovating and excavating sites on the island.

The first impressive feature of the town is the walls themselves. Complete except for one 20th-century entranceway, they sit strong and proud, especially beautiful at night when the soft glow of wrought-iron lamps reveals their rosy hue. The Knights did not begin the citadel from scratch; they developed a series of Byzantine defenses creating eight walls or 'curtains', each one the responsibility of a separate 'langue' or nationality that made up the order of the Knights *(see page 26)*. At one time each curtain had a gate, but today there are only seven original gates left, each with its own design; most are only wide enough to accept foot traffic. The most interesting gate is that of **d'Amboise** – situated in the northwest corner, it was built in 1512, during the reign of Grand Master Emery d'Amboise; it curves in an S-shape to outwit attackers and is then linked to a second gate, **St Anthony's**, which lies between two inner curtain walls. A walk around the outskirts of the walls will take about 40 minutes, but beware that if you walk in the moat area you might not be able to gain access to many of the gates as they sit high in the walls above with walkways across the moat.

In 1924 the Italians altered the Old Town walls and created an entrance for vehicles. This was when the motor vehicle was king, and it was clear that the traffic would need access along the waterfront. The raised and widened gate – christened Pýli Eleftherías, or **Freedom Gate** – cut St Paul's Gate and Bastion from the rest of the citadel and now sits seaside of the road. The creation of Freedom Gate also

A popular feature of Rhodes Old Town is the d'Amboise gate, one of seven remaining in the original Byzantine walls.

meant covering the moat that divided the inner and outer curtain at this point. Today most visitors enter the Old Town for the first time through this gate as it is the nearest to the taxi stand and main bus stations.

The freedom gate leads directly to the **Collachium** or Knights' Quarter, where the langues had their inns and the Grand Master had his Palace. Beyond this is the Bourg or town area where you'll find a fascinating maze of streets, comprising the Turkish quarter and the old Jewish sector of the town.

The Knights' Quarter

All the living and administrative quarters of the Knights can be found in the northernmost sector of the city. As you travel through Freedom Gate you'll find yourself in **Platía Sýmis** (Symi Square) and you'll see the remnants of the third-century BC **Temple of Aphrodite**. Only a few columns and a section of entablature are on view, though other remains were found behind the two bank buildings to your right. Next door to the banks is a small gallery displaying 20th-century art.

Walk beyond the temple to reach **Platía Argyrokástrou**, which is decorated by a fountain with a dolphin spout. The base of the fountain is in fact a Byzantine baptismal font discovered by Italian archaeologists in the south of the island but it doesn't look at all out of place here. The square is flanked on the east by the **Inn of Auvergne**, built in the 16th century for the 'langue of Auvergne' – one of several French-speaking langues within the

Knights' order. Behind the fountain is a building of 14th-century origin and thought to have been the original hospital for the order, although it was later used as an arsenal or **Armeria** – hence its modern official name. It is now used as the archive for the Institute of Archaeology for the Dodecanese. You'll find the **Decorative Arts Museum** in the south wing of the

The French-speaking knights found refuge at the Auberge d'Auvergne.

Armeria. This is comprised of an interesting collection of embroidery, weaving and wood carvings among other traditional arts. One section displays an entire Rhodian single-room house complete with household tools and accessories. All the traditional island handcrafts are on display here, and you can browse at your leisure and decide what appeals most before you shop in the bazaar area later in the day.

Make your way under the archway past the traffic control point and you will find yourself on the cobbled streets that characterise the Knights' Quarter. Ahead is **Platía Mousiou** (Museum Square), home to several important buildings. On your left is **Panagía tou Kástrou** (The Church of Our Lady of the Castle), built by the Byzantines and completed by the Knights, who made it into their cathedral. Its minimalist stone walls display 14th-century paintings that show it to be a Roman Catholic place of worship, though it was converted into a mosque during the Ottoman period. Rhodians call it the 'Red Church' because of massacres of Christians that took place here in the aftermath of the Great Siege. Today, the church is home to the **Museum of Religious Art in the Post-Byzantine Period**, displaying a collection of powerful icons, mostly from the 14th and 15th centuries but also some very modern interpretations of traditional religious themes. To the southeastern corner of the square is the **Inn of England** (1483), which was rebuilt by the Italians after being destroyed in 1856.

The western flank of the square is dominated by one of the most important buildings in the Old Town – the Knights' Hospital, which now houses the **Archaeological Museum of Rhodes**. This is an attraction of epic proportions since it not only houses finds from all the ancient sites on the island, but the building itself pays testament to the wealth of the Order of the Knights of St

The courtyard of Rhodes' Archaeological Museum hints at the treasures within.

John and to the considerable prowess of builders in the medieval period.

Construction of this 'new' hospital began in 1440 under the auspices of Jean Bonpart de Lastic. The plaque above the main entrance states that the previous Grand Master Fluvian bequeathed 10,000 gold florins for the building fund; however, it was not fully completed until 1489 under Grand Master d'Aubusson, whose plaque of recognition fronts Museum Square. Restoration has been ongoing since the Italian era and was needed following damage that occurred during World War II. The hospital was state-of-the-art for its time and its doctors treated Christians from around the world.

Inside the building is a large courtyard flanked by vaulted porticos and graced by a lion statue of Hellenistic origin. There are also piles of cannonballs from various sieges against the town, including those of Demetrius and Suleiman the Magnificent. To the left of the courtyard, a stone staircase leads to the infirmary room. A vast open space, with a roof supported by several stone columns, it gives the impression of a medieval courtroom. This was the main ward of the hospital with a capacity for over 100 beds and several small recessed rooms for the very sick. It had a fire at one end but very few other luxuries. Today, the room houses relics of the era of the knights. The gravestones of illustrious members are on display here, with coats-of-arms depicting several houses.

The rooms on the rest of the floor, including the large refectory, have been divided into smaller spaces to display Classical statuary and other artifacts found at Iálysos and Kámiros, as well as other sites on Rhodes, and also items from various islands in the Dodecanese. The rooms around the balcony house pottery. Rooms 6–8 display finds from Iálysos, which range from the 9th to the 4th century BC, while rooms 9–15 display finds from Kámiros. Both sites were excavated during the Italian period.

The atrium area to the north, the food preparation area of the hospital during the time of the knights, is home to some splendid Classical statuary and grave stelae. The grave stele of Krito and Tamerista is one of the most renowned exhibits. It was carved around 410 BC by a local artist, in the style prevalent in Athens at that time, and was found at Kámiros. Nearby is a kouros dating from the Archaic period, and there is a small head of Zeus found near his Temple on Mount Attávyros. Other rooms display extremely fine Hellenistic

Oh Deer

Prompted by the Delphic oracle deer were introduced to Rhodes during ancient times to combat the island's snakes, which were said to be repelled by their odour. In the modern era, the deer died out, but the island was re-stocked by the Italians during the 1920s and '30s. As for the snakes – the Delphic oracle was clearly misinformed regarding reptiles, and there is still a shy and elusive population in remote parts of the island.

and Roman statuary including a marble work entitled Aphrodite of Rhodes, with the goddess crouched and fanning out her hair. This was carved in the 1st century BC but considered to be a copy of a 3rd-century BC work.

Where the rooms regale us with well-chosen, well-displayed statuary, the atrium garden has an eclectic and haphazard collection of items that are fun to discover. Sections of columns and the remains of a large carved dolphin, perhaps once part of a fountain, rest between the potted plants.

When you have finished exploring the museum, turn left out of the entrance and left again to view one of the most complete medieval streets in the world. This is **Odós Ippotón** (Street of the Knights), where many of the Inns of the Order were based. Its buildings are of finely chiselled sandstone offering one long façade that rises to a double archway, which spans the road at its peak. Small square windows and fine arched doorways break the walls of stone – doors wide enough for horse and carriage or a single rider atop his steed. When the Italians took control of the island, the street was in a bad state of repair, and the Turks had added Ottoman windows to the upper floors. These were removed and a careful restoration carried out ,which was complete by 1916.

Take a stroll along Ippotón to admire each building in turn; there are many small details to be seen, including fine carved stonemasonry and commemorative plaques. The first building you pass on the right is the **Inn of Italy**, with a plaque honouring 16th-century Grand Master Fabrizio del Carretto above its entranceway. Next to it is the smaller **Palace of Villiers de l'Isle-Adam**, the immediate successor of Carretto, and the Grand Master ignominiously ousted by

Odós Ippotón leads a curious traveller back to the Middle Ages – the medieval street has been carefully restored.

Suleiman in 1522. Across the street was another entrance to the Infirmary now barred with an iron gate. On the same side, but higher up, you'll see a small garden decorated with an Ottoman fountain, which is part of the museum complex. Cross the street to the **Inn of France** where a splendid life-

Enclave of the Knights

In their Rhodes bastion the Knights, all members of the noblest families in Europe, took monastic vows of obedience, poverty and chastity. Seven *langues* or 'tongues' were represented according to native language; these were English, German, French, Provençal, Auvergnat, Spanish and Italian. Each *langue* lived in a compound called an inn, under an appointed prior. For security, they went about in pairs and left the walled domain only on horseback.

French influence outweighed the other tongues when it came to electing the lifelong post of Grand Master. Thus, 14 of the 19 Grand Masters were French, and French was the order's spoken language (Latin for official documents). The Italians' natural maritime talents made them the obvious choice to command the fleet, while other tongues each defended a section, or 'curtain', of the city walls.

Following their departure from Rhodes, the knights were without a base for eight years. Eventually, the island of Malta was offered to them by Charles V, Holy Roman Emperor. In 1530, they changed their name to the Knights of Malta and stayed on the island for 268 years until Napoleon invaded in 1798 and ordered them to leave.

Today the order is still in existence, with numerous 'branches' of the peaceful and charitable associations in Britain and the United States. They have also rented back part of their old Maltese stronghold.

sized carving of a knight in repose is set in stone – perhaps once a tombstone – just inside the courtyard. The Inn of France is the most highly decorated of the inns, and its internal courtyard has a chapel dating from the era of Raymond Béranger, who was Grand Master from 1365–74, though the street frontage dates from over 100 years later. At the top of Ippotón are two final inns, those of **Provence** (1418), on the right, and **Spain**, on the left, which housed two separate langues, those of Aragon and Castile. Beyond the Inn of Spain are the remains of the **Church of St John of the Collachium**, named after the Orders patron. This is where the Grand Masters were buried. The Ottomans used its basement as a gunpowder magazine, and there was a powerful explosion in 1856 that destroyed the church and damaged many surrounding buildings.

During the daytime you will find Ippotón crowded with visitors strolling along, or large tour groups striding to the next location on the itinerary. This may make it difficult to imagine the knights arriving on horseback, walking between inns for strategy meetings or rabble-rousing, or heading to the infirmary to attend to their medical duties. At night the street takes on a quieter, more magical atmosphere with the waxy glow of the streetlights reminiscent of the oil lamps that would have burned there centuries ago. At this time of day it is possible to imagine yourself back in the 14th century among this small band of soldier/medics on an outpost far from home.

On the right at the top of Odós Ippotón you will have your first glimpse of the **Palace of the Grand Master**. This was the administrative heart and power base of the Order of the Knights of St John and the most important building in the Knights' Quarter. Left to fall into a state of disrepair by the Ottomans – they used it as a prison before the explosion of 1856 left it badly damaged – it was renovated by the Italians

Many of the elaborate mosaics found in the Grand Master's Palace come from the neighbouring island of Kos.

with a result that is still controversial to this day for a number of reasons. The original plans for the palace were not adhered to in the renovations, thus the interior has many features added with a modern eye. Statuary and mosaics found within the walls come mainly from neighbouring islands whose populations still suffer from the loss of some of their finest relics. Finally, Greek archaeologists would have preferred to demolish the ruins of the palace to excavate the site in search of a Classical temple thought to lie directly beneath. However the Italians saw the opportunity of creating an impressive summer palace for their royal family (later for dictator Benito Mussolini), and so the palace was rebuilt.

Despite these controversies, the building is not a disappointment. The renovations were undertaken by mastercraftsmen, and the structure retains a majesty that befits its old role. Columns and capitals from ancient sites have been used throughout the interior, and the smooth stonework shows what the whole of the Knights' Quarter would have looked like when newly built. Look for the magnificent wooden ceilings, and the panes of onyx in the windows that let in a soft translucent light. Many of the major rooms have beautiful Hellenistic, Roman and early-Christian mosaics taken from sites across Kos, a neighbouring Dodecanese island. Although it is ethically questionable whether they should be here, they have been carefully preserved and look spectacular.

Enter the palace between two imposing semi-circular towers. The rooms now open to the public are on the upper floor and reached by a grand marble staircase. They are airy although sparsely furnished to allow a better appreciation of the structure and mosaics. The latter include examples depicting the Nine Muses, one with a nymph on a sea-horse, and another showing the Head of the Medusa; fish and dolphins are also popular themes.

The ground floor rooms, which originally acted as

Countless visitors pour through the grand entrance of the Palace.

stables and as grain and munitions stores through the great sieges, are reached across the courtyard sporting a series of Classical statues. The rooms house a permanent exhibition of finds from 2,400 years of Rhodes' history, and there are temporary exhibitions.

On leaving the palace compound turn right and walk across the square now used for parking to reach Odós Orféos. Here an avenue of plane trees offers some shade and there are several tavernas with tourist menus. A right turn at Orféos leads through **St Anthony's Gate**, where you have the opportunity to walk down to the moat or defensive ditch area (since this area was never filled with water it is technically wrong to call it a moat). Or move on to **d'Amboise Gate**, where you'll find several artists in the shade offering to paint your portrait. A short walk across its span will lead you into Rhodes New Town from where you can turn and admire the walls, gate and Palace. This is truly one of the most impressive views of the citadel and Knights' Quarter.

The Chora or Bourg

Only the Knights were allowed to live with the Collachium, although the rest of the population lived within the city walls. When the Turks arrived, only they and the Jews lived in the citadel, and the town took on a new image as mosques replaced churches and the Ottoman penchant for trade saw the development of a large bazaar. Though many buildings of Turkish origin were destroyed in the aftermath of their departure, the Old Town still has fascinating corners to explore. There is a maze of stone alleyways leading to hidden corners – some will be busy with people, others will be deserted. The delight of exploring this part of the Old Town is that you don't know what's around the next bend, yet no matter where you wander you can't get lost – you'll always be secure within those strong high walls.

The Chora has shops, cafés and restaurants galore, so if you are looking for some retail therapy or a cooling drink after enjoying all the museums then this is the place to be.

From the entrance to the palace walk straight ahead on Odós Panetíou. The faded rose-tinted walls and distinctive minaret of the **Mosque of Suleiman** can be seen on the right. The mosque, built in 1523 to mark the Ottoman takeover of the island,has been under renovation for many years but this is now nearing completion. Sadly, it is still only possible to view this important monument from the outside. Climb the small flight of steps to the right before

A lasting reminder of the Ottoman Empire, the Mosque of Suleiman stands out among historical Rhodes architecture.

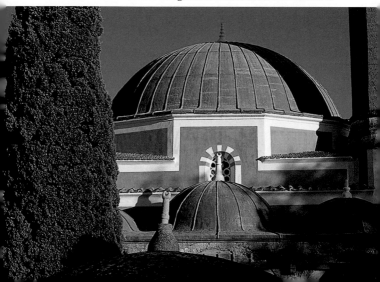

you reach the mosque. This gives you the best views of the large dome that tops the building. This alleyway also leads to the **To Roloï**, a clock tower erected in 1851. Climb to the top (small admission fee) for some of the most impressive views over the rooftops of the Old Town. From here you can clearly see what a maze it is and yet how small an area it covers.

Panetiou terminates at **Odós Sokrátous** (Socrates Street), the main shopping thoroughfare of the Turkish Quarter in Ottoman times, as well as in the present day. Before you stroll past the tempting wares, the building on the corner of Sokrátous and Odós Ipodamou is worth noting. This is a **Muslim library**, founded in 1794; it houses a number of rare handwritten Korans dating from the 15th and 16th centuries along with Arab and Persian manuscripts, all of which form a priceless collection. The elegant Arabic script carved around the doorway will tell you that you are in the right place.

At first glance Socrates Street is just as it was one hundred and fifty years ago – hundreds of people bargaining for goods in many languages, shopkeepers eager for business but willing to do a little bartering in order to get the sale. Of course times have changed: electricity, glass windows and the constant ring of portable telephones confirm that you're in the 21st century. T-shirts weren't quite so *de rigueur* all those years ago, but there is still the palpable feeling of the old bazaar in these streets. Few visitors seem to leave empty-handed, perhaps owing to the range and quality of goods on offer here, or maybe since the skillful sales pitch breaks down all resistance.

Socrates has a good range of stores along its length, from high-quality shops selling designer watches and gem-encrusted jewellery to vendors selling copies of designer-wear, kitsch remembrances or tacky postcards. Little alleyways strewn with wares leading left and right off Socrates lead on to other alleyways, and so it continues – your money may well run out before the shopping opportunities do.

Take a detour on any of the alleyways to the south (right) of Socrates into what was the residential sector of the **Turkish Quarter**, perhaps the most intriguing area in the town. Narrow twisting alleyways lead to empty squares, disused and dilapidated mosques, Neo-Classical façades, Ottoman wooden balconies and a myriad of earthy shades of stucco finishing the walls. Stone archways spanning the lanes, though aesthetically pleasing, also have a serious purpose, ie to provide structural support in the event of an earthquake. In the evenings, as the street lights flicker and every taverna sets up three or four tables in the street, this area seems to awaken from a deep sleep. Take your time to explore here – streets such as Agiou Fanouriou, Pythagora and Sofokleous make good starting points, and if you begin to feel jaded try a Turkish bath at the renovated **Mustafa Pasha** *hammam* on Platía Aríonos next to the faded glory that was the **Mosque of Sultan Mustafa Pasha**.

The bottom of Socrates will bring you to **Platía Ippokrátous** (Hippocrates Square), one of the main meeting places in the Old Town, only a little way south of **Sea Gate** with its massive towers. In the centre of the square is the **Syntrivani**, a fountain topped by a miniature minaret and normally bedecked by pigeons. In the southeastern corner of the square, the stone building called the **Castellanía** was the medieval courthouse and stock exchange of the knights, completed in 1507. The building now houses the public library and town archives.

Hippocrates Square is one of the primary gathering spots in the Old Town and a great place to meet friends.

You can then stroll on to Odós Aristotélous until you reach **Platía Evréon Martýron** (Square of the Martyrs). This is the old **Jewish Quarter** of the town, and the square is named in remembrance of those rounded up and killed by German soldiers during World War II. Of the 2,000 that were here when the Germans arrived in 1943, only 50 returned after the war. At the centre of the square there is a fountain decorated with bronze seahorses. On the north side of the square is the old Naval Headquarters for the knights; this became the seat of Orthodoxy for Rhodes and is now known as the **Archbishop's Palace**. The **Kal de Shalom Synagogue**, on Odós Dosiádou, just off the square, was built in the 16th century and has been carefully renovated with funds sent by ex-patriot Jewish Rhodians.

As you stroll towards the city gate that leads to the commercial harbour you'll see the ruined **Church of Our Lady of the Bourg**. Only the Gothic three-tiered apse remains.

New Town

During the Turkish occupation, the Greek population and others who were not allowed to live in the Old Town inhabited the area immediately outside the city walls. When the Italians took control of the island, they set about putting their mark on Rhodes by redeveloping the New Town with modern administrative buildings, churches and office buildings. Rhodes Town is the capital of the Dodecanese group of Greek islands and many important official activities take place here just as they did during Italian jurisdiction. Unfortunately, the architectural style in vogue at the time has

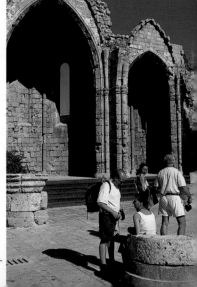

fallen from favour – dour bland industrial façades that make many of the New Town's public buildings rather forgettable. What draws locals and visitors alike is the range of eateries, bars and clubs here, which give the area lots of energy well into the night.

As you emerge from the Old Town the waters of **Mandráki Harbour** are a natural draw. This large

Little is left of the Church of Our Lady of the Bourg, but the ruins are lovely.

harbour was once the main port for the ancient city. In the summer, it is home to numerous colourful tour boats, which ply their routes down the coast to Líndos, or to nearby islands. The western side has berths for numerous private sailboats from around Europe and is a hang-out for US and Australian ex-pats. Around the harbour wall are the remains of three windmills, while **St Nicholas Fort**, with its eponymous chapel dedicated to the patron saint of sailors, sits at the seaward end. The fort acts as a lighthouse for modern vessels manoeuvering these busy shallows. Mandráki harbourfront is a favourite spot for Rhodians to take their regular *volta* (evening stroll).

Head north following the harbour's path, and across the four-lane highway you'll see **Rimini Square** with its seemingly constant chaotic traffic. The main taxi stand is here, as, behind it, is the municipal tourism office. Through a wide gateway leading to the dry defensive moat of the Old Town is the entrance to the **Sound and Light Show**, which takes place nightly in summer. The spectacle takes you back to the Great Siege of Suleiman the Magnificent with a cacophony of sound and dazzling illumination, bringing the events that have marked the stone walls to life.

Across Rimini Square is the **Néa Agorá** (New Market), built by the Italians in Oriental style on the site of a much older market. This seems to form a focus of much activity with both main bus 'stations' nearby. On the seafront façade, excellent *zacharoplastia* (pastry shops) tempt you with succulent delicacies, while the landward façades have shops selling Rhodian and Cretan specialities such as honey and dried fruits. This is the place to come for delicious gyros and

Take a scenic stroll along the waterfront – a rustic seaside sight is the windmill on Mandráki Harbour.

budget tavernas, intermingled with high-value jewellery stores and kitsch souvenir emporia.

As you continue strolling along the harbour you'll see its distinctive entrance come into view. For many years it was thought that the Colossus stood astride the approach, but modern scientists have concluded that the underlying ground would not have supported the weight of such a large edifice. Two columns now frame the opening, topped by two bronze statues known as **the Platoní**. One is a bronze doe; the other is a stag.

Alongside the harbour mouth is the **Church of St John**, the most important church on the island and seat of the Archbishop of the Dodecanese; unfortunately, its rather dull façade is a poor replacement for the old Church of St John of the Collachium. Inland from the church are the main administrative buildings built by the Italians: the **Governor's Palace**, the **Town Hall** and **National Theatre**.

Continue northward and walk towards the minaret straight ahead. This is the highest part of the **Murad Reis Mosque**, which is now looking rather forlorn and neglected. Peer through the wrought-iron railings at the exquisitely carved tumbledown headstones of the old cemetery. Murad Reis was a famed Turkish buccaneer who met his end during the 1522 siege when acting as one of Suleiman's admirals. He is buried in the circular mausoleum at the side of the mosque.

Beyond the mosque is **Elli**, the main town beach, and, at the northern tip of the island just a couple of hundred yards away, is the **Aquarium** or Enydrío, run by the Hydrobiological Institute. Many of the creatures on display are native to the seas around Rhodes.

South of Mandráki Harbour you can continue to walk along the waterside through **St Paul's Gate**, an outer defensive bastion of the Old Town, to reach **Emborio**, the commercial

Extravagant yachts outnumber the humble fishing boats in Mandráki Harbour, where the ex-pats gather in droves.

harbour that is always busy with the movements of a colourful fishing fleet, cruise ships, commercial ferries and merchantmen. There is a narrow stretch of sand here often used by ferry passengers before they embark on the long journey back to Piraeus. You'll also find one of the most dramatic entrances to the Citadel, the **Sea Gate**, flanked by two large round towers. As you pass through it look up between the walls to see the remnants of the mechanisms that operated the gate and imagine all the people who have walked on that same spot since the Middle Ages.

Much of modern Rhodes Town sprawls out southwest of the Old and New Towns. Just 2 km (about 1 mile) from the walls of the Old Town the high ground of **Monte Smith**, 110 m (365 ft), offers a good overview of the whole settlement. Walk

The stoic remains of the Temple of Apollo stand high atop Monte Smith.

east from the d'Amboise Gate or take bus no. 5, which passes the site. The Italians named Monte Smith after Sir Sydney Smith, a 19th-century British Admiral who established a lookout point here to watch the French fleet marshalling for an attack on Ottoman territory. In addition to the view of Rhodes, her surrounding islands and the Turkish coast, you will also find the remains of the Doric **Temple of Apollo**. Three columns have been re-erected by the Italians – part of ancient Rhodes and proof that this city was far larger than the Rhodes of today.

Below the temple are the scant remains of an ancient theatre and sporting stadium. Monte Smith offers great views of the sunset, which makes it a favourite spot for romantic young couples to gather in the evenings.

If you need some cooling shade after a few hours of sightseeing, then try a visit to **Rodini Park** 3 km (2 miles) south of the Old Town. The smell of fragrant pine fills this wooded parkland, where the knights used to cultivate medicinal herbs, and you can hear the calls of the resident peacocks. There are walkways through the trees and around a small lake. Scholars say that this was the site of the famed

School of Oratory in ancient times. Today, it plays host to numerous festivals throughout the year.

THE EAST COAST

The East coast of Rhodes is sheltered from the prevailing winds blowing down through the Aegean. Its coastline is an interesting mix of wide sandy bays and small sandy coves, with high hills interrupting the flow of the main coastal road. Several resorts sit along the coast and there are numerous excursions into the hills.

Travelling south from Rhodes, the first resort is **Kallithéa**, which sprang up around the Italian thermal centre of **Kallithéa Spa** 6 km (4 miles) from Rhodes. You can still visit the decidedly Moorish spa buildings with their tiles and domed roof, though they now stand neglected and careworn. The Italian hope of creating competition for spas in Switzerland and Czechoslovakia never came to fruition.

Inland from Kallithéa, the village of **Koskinoú** was once inhabited solely by Turks. The village is now one of the most unusual on the island, with its traditional 17th- and 18th-century Rhodian houses are kept in pristine condition. Every door and window-frame receives a regular treatment of bright

The place to go if you love to party – Faliráki Beach is a popular hot-spot.

paint, and the whole effect is enhanced with potted plants in ceramic pots.

From Kallithéa Spa continue along the coast road and you'll soon go around the headland into Kallithéa Bay. This is one of the best beaches on the island and it's no surprise that it has been exploited for tourism. On the south side of the bay is **Faliráki**, one of the hottest spots in Europe for young, fun-loving sun worshippers. By day Faliráki is low key. Most activity takes place around the beach where you can enjoy watersports, bungy-jumping, waterslides or just lying under one of the thousands of umbrellas that line the strand. As the sun sets and the neon lights are switched on, those of a nervous disposition should leave town. Bars compete to see which can play their music the loudest, and who can create a cocktail with the most alcohol. It's great fun for some, but it's definitely not for everyone.

Nearby **Ladikó Bay** is also known as Zorba's Beach – given

this name by local villagers when Anthony Quinn (star of *Zorba the Greek*) came here to film *The Guns of Navarone*.

Afántou is the next major settlement. It lies in the middle of a long bay of the same name. Just as you enter the bay you'll see signs for the only 18-hole golf course on Rhodes, though the greens have a decidedly brown

At Eptá Pigés, you can sit and listen to the waterfalls splash on the rocks.

appearance, and the fairways are said to be extra firm. The word Afántou means *invisible* and refers to the fact that the village cannot be seen from the sea because it lies in a hollow a little way inland. This protected it from pirates and, later, from Turkish raids. The people have cultivated orchards of soft fruits such as apricots for many generations, and their women are highly praised for their carpet weaving, a tradition that continues into the 21st century. From Afántou it is possible to travel inland to Petaloúdhes (Valley of the Butterflies) via the village of Psínthos – this attraction is described on page 61.

The crossroads at **Kolýmbia** offers you the opportunity to turn left to the pretty coastal resort of the same name. There is a tiny fishing harbour on the southern side. Or you can turn inland to **Eptá Pigés** (Seven Springs) for the perfect antidote to those hot dry summer days in town or on the beach.

Seven Springs is indeed a source of fresh water, which has been exploited by farmers for centuries. The water provided sustenance for crops, and a verdant pine forest with numerous species of wild orchids, which the Italians developed to create a recreational woodland. Italian engineers managed the water supply and created an artificial lake in the middle of the forest, with footpaths through the countryside. Most visitors seem to enjoy following the springs from their origin, down through the artificial conduits and into a large pipe cut under a nearby hillside to the site of the lake. You can navigate the nearly 200-m- (600-ft-) long tunnel with the aid of a torch, but watch out for people coming back in the other direction – it's not really made for two-way traffic. Of course you don't have to attempt this 'pot-holing' exercise. You can take one of the footpaths overland or just sit at the café in the cooling shade of the forest and watch the ducks, geese and peacocks go about their

Enjoy the view down to the beach at Tsambíka Bay from the cliff up above.

business. Once you get settled at Seven Springs you may not want to leave.

Your rest should have replenished your energy for the climb to the **Monastery of Panagía Tsambíka**, situated at the peak of a rocky hill overlooking the coast just a little further south. Many people walk from the main road, especially the female pilgrims who travel to the church on 8 September each year to pray for fertility and the chance of a child. Though modern fertility treatments have lowered their numbers, you may hear children called Tsambíka if a girl or Tsambíkos if a boy – a sure sign that the Virgin answered a mother's prayer. Even if you drive up to the parking lot near the monastery there are still 298 steps to the pinnacle, a walk that literally takes your breath away. Once there, the church itself is disappointing, but the views definitely are not. Three hundred and twenty six m (1070 ft) directly below is the sandy **Bay of Tsambíka**. Beyond this, several bays are visible as far as Líndos, and lines of rugged cliffs and peaks fill the panorama.

Archángelos is one of the largest villages on the island and has made a living independent of tourism – through farming and ceramics, for which it is well regarded. There are several 'factories' here, and many display their wares at roadside outlets. On a rocky bluff above the village you'll see the remains of a knight's castle that once offered protection to the citizens. Archángelos is also one of the few places where the traditional leather boots worn by farmers are still made by hand using the most supple hides. The high cut was essential to protect against a snake bite in days when these creatures were much more numerous. From Archángelos you can make the short journey east to the small beach at **Stegná**. There is a burgeoning resort here but it is not, as yet, overdeveloped.

Heading south, the road moves inland to avoid the towering peak of **Profítis Ilías**. Make the left turn to the village of **Charáki**, where you can enjoy the best seafood on the island at one of the several tavernas lining the seafront. After lunch, head up above the village to explore **Faraklós Castle**, one of the largest on the island after the capital citadel. Little remains of the castle today but in its heyday it must have been impressive – it was the last to fall to Ottoman forces in the 1520s, holding out long after Rhodes itself had fallen. The track leading to the castle also leads to **Agáthi Beach** a little further north. Perhaps the prettiest on Rhodes, Agáthi is the destination for many small boats *(caïques)* from Líndos and Rhodes Town – it's perfect for swimming and snorkelling and has three good bars for refreshment.

The main road travels across the wide Mássari Plain on its way to Líndos. Here, among the crops of tomatoes and 'greens', you'll see the remains of an old airfield used by German forces during World War II. Eventually, after travelling through **Kálathos** village, you go around a rocky outcrop to gain your first view of the citadel and village of Líndos. There is a vantage point on the roadside here, where you can stop and take photographs.

The whitewashed buildings of the town of Líndos are cosily nestled below the site of the Líndos Acropolis.

LÍNDOS

In ancient times **Líndos** was the most cosmopolitan and commercial of the three city states on the island. The city had a 'golden age' in the 6th century BC under its ruler Kleoboulos, who was considered one of the 'seven sages' of the ancient world. It was he who established the Temple of Athena at the site. This temple sanctuary allowed Líndos to remain viable even after the founding of ancient Rhodes Town in 408 BC, as it was the most important religious site on the island.

Set high upon a towering coastal precipice it was seen as a strategic strong point throughout history, and the Byzantines and knights both fortified the site before it fell into gentle decline during Ottoman rule (save for a few sea captains who made money plying the Mediterranean Sea). They built fine strong houses, which now form the backbone of the town below the citadel. Líndos was a backwater until the 1960s, when hippies decided it was the place to hang out; soon the fashionable set followed, and money rolled in to renovate the buildings and create a whitewashed 'picture perfect' settlement.

Today the town presents something of an enigma. One of the most-photographed locations in Greece, it has a permanent population of under 1,000 people. Tourism is its lifeblood yet it still retains a strong character and atmosphere beyond its tourist face. If possible, arrive early when you can wander in peace and see the simple beauty of the architecture.

Most vehicles are banned from the village, so your bus or taxi will drop you in the tiny main square. From here a maze of narrow streets criss-cross the lower hill with shops selling art and handcrafts, bars offering cocktails and restaurants with roof gardens tempting you up for a bird's-eye view. Líndos is one place on Rhodes where you can still find the traditional one-room house – given by a girl's family as a dowry on her marriage. Surrounded by high walls these homes had small outer courtyards whose floors were laid with a mosaic of pebbles or *hochlákia*, and often shaded by a canopy of vines. Today, many are holiday studios managed under the auspices of European package tour operators. The **Captain's or Patrician houses** have mostly been converted into restaurants or bars. The best example – appropriately called the Captain's House – has been lovingly restored by its French owner. It's a classical music bar – a soothing contrast to the many rock bars in town.

As you follow the hand-painted signs for the Acropolis sitting high above the village, look for a small red-roofed church on your left. This is the 15th-century **Panagía**

Much like the Acropolis in Athens, the Líndos site requires stamina for the climb.

(Church of the Assumption of Our Lady), decorated with late Byzantine frescoes by Gregory of Symi. Take note of the pretty floor of patterned *hochlákia*.

The climb to the Acropolis is steep but steady, made worse in summer by the hot air that hangs heavy in the streets. You can take a donkey ride to the top – the station is by the main square – for only a few euros. These are just about the only working donkeys left on the island, as so many have been usurped by modern farming machinery in the fields.

If you walk, as you leave the village behind you'll find women laying their lace and cotton wares out against the rocks, tempting you to make a purchase. Take time to look across the rooftops below and on to the curved bay with its bobbing caïques offering trips along the coast and expensive motor launches moored offshore. The sea has an azure hue and it looks very inviting.

Ahead you'll see the Byzantine and medieval walls of the **Acropolis** looming large. The ticket office sits just inside the lower gate of the citadel and then you must climb a monumental staircase to reach the pinnacle – the main part of the site. Before you start to climb look for the **relief of a**

Greek *trireme* or warship on the rocks to your left. The steps are steep with no handrail, so do take care.

At the top of the steps you enter the **Commander's Palace**, which is connected to several administrative buildings used by the knights. Once out onto the pinnacle, on your left are the remains of the Byzantine **Church of Ayios Ioannis** (St John). Pass through the dark chambers near the church to reach the base of the **Sanctuary of Athena Lindia**.

Here you'll be confronted with a large **Hellenistic stoa** (covered walkway) 87 m (285 ft) long and constructed around 200 BC, which would have contained shops selling offerings to take into the sanctuary. Once on top of the stoa, climb the wide staircase in the centre to the **propylaia** – the entrance to the sanctuary itself. This consisted of a series of further stoas, which shielded the most sacred part of the sanctuary at the highest sea-

As picturesque as one can imagine, a typical house in Líndos offers a perfect photo opportunity.

View the ornate interior of the church of Kimísis Theotókou in Asklepio.

ward point on the rock. The remains seen today date from the Hellenistic era – circa mid-4th century BC; the sanctuary of Kleoboulos was destroyed by fire in 392 BC. These include several columns of the propylaia and inner sanctuary *bemas* (raised platforms).

Surrounding the site are the 14th-century walls built by the knights. These offer panoramic views across **Líndos Bay** to the north, the town to the west with scant remains of a Roman theatre, and tiny rocky **St Paul's Bay** to the south. This was where St Paul was said to have landed when thrown off course by a fierce storm in AD 51. The gap in the rocks here is said to have miraculously opened, allowing his boat to land safely. A small, whitewashed church now marks the spot.

SOUTH FROM LÍNDOS

You'll find the village of **Lárdos** inland from Líndos. It is a thriving farming community with a few tourist shops and is worth a visit for its different ambiance to its near neighbour. Inland from Lárdos it is 12 km (6½ miles) to the village of **Láerma** where you can take to the hills on a number of foot and donkey tracks. This part of the island has lost its younger population to the coastal resorts where there is employment and excitement, leaving the older folks to tend crops and spend days crocheting or chatting over coffee at the *kafeníon*. Begun in the 9th century, the Monastery of **Moní Thári** is the oldest on Rhodes. It is located just south of Láerma. Before setting off on the unsurfaced road, find a caretaker for the church in the village because it is not open at regular hours. Your effort will be rewarded with stunning frescoes dating from the 12th to the 16th centuries.

On the coast at Lárdos Bay is the small resort of **Péfkos**. Its sandy beach makes it a popular choice with tourists and it has a growing number of souvenir shops. South from Péfkos the hotels and apartment buildings peter out, and the island takes on a wilder atmosphere. Villages are few and there are several ranges of barren hills rising over 500 m (1640 ft).

Make a right turn to the village of **Asklipió**, nestled in the lea of Mount Troulia and protected in medieval times by a knight's castle. Here, it is said, was the birthplace of Asklepios, Greek god of healing, and in ancient times there was an important therapeutic centre here. Initiates at the centre functioned as both healers and priests, attracting pilgrims from around the Greek world. Today Asklipió is one of the most traditional villages on Rhodes, where donkeys stand tethered in doorways ready to carry farmers to nearby fields and women still bake bread every morning in backyard wood-burning ovens. Despite its muted atmosphere it still has treasures to reveal. Explore the remains of the castle if you have the energy to climb through the village, and then the scant remains of the ancient site. Following this, visit the small church in the centre of the village, which is a little gem. The **Monastery of Metamórfosi**, or Kímisis Theotókou, was built in the 11th century and is a beautiful example of Byzantine

When the wind occasionally whips off the Aegean, you will be grateful for the weighted pebbles on the beach at Ixiá.

design. Every nook and cranny of the interior is decorated with rich frescoes mostly added in the 15th century depicting biblical images and scenes of life under the knights.

Equidistant between the two coastlines in the south of the island is the village of **Messanagrós**, best reached from the east coast via **Lachaniá**. Nearby you'll find the **Monastery of Moni Skiádi**, which protects one of the most revered religious relics on the island: a miraculous icon of the Virgin Mary. The icon is paraded here each 8 September on the festival celebrating the Virgin's birth.

The far south of Rhodes used to be the realm of die hard explorers and windsurfers, who gathered at Prasonísi to hang out away from the world. However, a new tarmac road has opened the area to normal vehicles – travel time from Líndos is now around 30 minutes non-stop – so it can now be included on everyone's itinerary. **Prasonísi** is the place where the Aegean Sea to the north meets the Mediterranean Sea to the south. The southernmost part of Rhodes is a small island linked to the mainland by a shallow bank of sand. It's always windy here, with the prevailing 'northerlies' skimming across the beach and offshore to the south. This is the reason that Prasonísi is known worldwide by the windsurfing set. Throughout the summer there is a permanent population taking to the waves, and the speeds they reach are pretty impressive; however, they often camp here (illegally) to be as close to the water as possible, which can leave the area unkempt and littered.

THE WEST COAST

For the most part, the western coast of Rhodes is not as stimulating or picturesque as the east. The beaches are not as wide, and the prevailing winds and tides carry debris down the Aegean and deposit it directly on the shoreline. However, there are a number of interesting attractions to explore and the resort facilities in the northwest – close to Rhodes Town – are some of the best on the island.

Paradísi Airport lies on the coast 16 km (10 miles) south of Rhodes Town, and there are several villages along the route. However, as the number of hotels has grown over the last 30 years, these separate settlements seem, to the uninitiated eye, to blend into one resort 'strip'. First there is **Ixiá**, the most-established tourist area, with several large and luxurious hotels. This is not a true village in the sense that it has never had a permanent native population. Further south, **Triánta**, **Kremastí** and **Paradísi** have developed due to tourism but still have Greek domestic activities in addition to a tourist identity. From Triánta and Kremastí it is easy to travel inland to visit the remains of one of the most important settlements of ancient Rhodes, the citadel of **Ialysós**.

Unfortunately there is little left of the city that formed one arm of a powerful triumvirate with Kámiros and Líndos during the 1st millennium BC – though it was once so extensive that it stretched down the hillside to the coast. Its location, on high ground overlooking Rhodes Town, made it a prime strategic position during times of conflict – it was from here that the Knights consolidated their initial hold on the island in 1309, and also from here that Suleiman wrested it from their control in 1522. It was also a target for building stone as the newer settlement expanded. Stone was also taken to erect the other main attraction here, the **Monastery of Filérimos**, built on the site of an ancient temple to Zeus.

The Monastery has had a chequered life. Revered by Orthodox Christians, it was used as stables by the Ottomans and bombed by German forces during World War II. Today, its tranquil dignity shines through, and it's well worth spending a few moments in quiet reflection among the pines. The most impressive building on the site is the 14th-century **Church of Our Lady of Filérimos**, which houses four separate chapels within its walls. One was funded by Grand Master Emery d'Aubusson and bears his name. The cruciform baptismal font in the innermost chapel dates from the 6th century, though the stone used was originally part of the Classical temple – illustrating the numerous rebirths of the site.

At the threshold of the church look for the entrance to the subterranean Byzantine **Chapel of Ayios Georgios**, which is decorated with 16th-century frescoes. Beyond this are the scant remains of a Classical **Temple to Athena Polias and Zeus Polinieus**. Several cloisters of the monastery have been renovated and decorated with modern icons of colourful tesserae.

Outside the site entrance, look for signs to a 4th-century-BC **Doric fountain**, which came to light after a landslide in 1926. The footpath to the fountain is not secure; be certain that it has been opened to the public before walking that way. Even if you can't visit the fountain, take a stroll down the pine-shaded avenue with a series of bronze reliefs depicting the **Stations of the Cross** until you reach a huge cross perched atop the 265-m (875-ft) hillside. From here there are panoramic views south either from the lookout at the base of the cross or from the top of the cross itself.

Once past the airport at Paradísi, development peters out, and there are occasional beaches signposted right from the main road through grassland or fields. These will be quieter than beaches in the main resorts except at weekends, when local families take a break from town life. Look for a left turn up into the hills to **Petaloúdhes.** This name literally translates to 'butterflies', but the area is usually known in English as the Val-

ley of the Butterflies, and it's one of the prettiest spots on the island. The valley is one of the last locations with a thriving forest of liquid-amber trees that secrete a sticky resin once used to manufacture frankincense. The resin is one of the main food supplies for *Callimorpha quadripunctaria* – not a butterfly but the Jersey tiger moth, which gather in

Moths are actually what predominate in the lovely Valley of the Butterflies.

their hundreds of thousands here in the breeding season between May and September.

The whole valley has been well landscaped for visitors who can walk through the trees and over streams and around ponds and waterfalls, watching for their first sight of the moths. At first they are impossible to see, but as your eyes grow accustomed to their camouflage, you'll suddenly discover hundreds resting just a stone's throw away from you. The moths got their Latin name from the four spots visible when their wings are open, augmented by a dazzling flash of vivid pink. When they are at rest they display a dull chocolate-and-cream coat, much less interesting and difficult to see. The temptation is therefore to encourage them to take to the air in great numbers by making a sudden loud sound or vibration. However, let's not forget that these creatures are sleeping during the day and too much human interference will drive them away. The park has strict rules against deliberately disturbing them.

The climb to the top of the valley takes about one hour, and you can exit to view the tiny whitewashed 18th-century chapel of **Kalópetra**, with its ornate frescoes, before taking to the cool, shady trail for the walk back down. For those with an insatiable love of animals there is an ostrich farm signposted off

Besides butterflies, the valley also features the quaint chapel of Kalópetra.

the Petaloúdhes road a couple of kilometres (about a mile) before you reach the butterflies.

The coastal road leads on south, with the looming peak of **Mount Profítis Ilías** rising inland to 789 m (2,617 ft). This is a beautiful peak to explore, blanketed in a pine forest that fills the air with its heady fragrance and provides a carpet of spiny leaves underfoot. There are two hotels among the trees built in the style of Alpine ski lodges, a small chapel dedicated to Elijah (Profítis Ilías), and numerous footpaths through the countryside. From the village of **Sálakos** to the north you can take the old donkey trail up the mountain. Unfortunately, the summit is off-limits, as the Greek military has a base there.

While exploring this area, take a trip to the tiny Byzantine chapel of **St Nicholas Fountouklís**, near the village of **Eleoúsa**. Once part of a larger monastery complex, the four-apsed structure has some beautiful 14th-century frescoes. The chapel is dedicated to a family of three children (all plague victims) and was paid for by their father who survived them.

Further south the coast road passes through farmland where the crops change with the season; however, there's little else of interest until you come to the site of the ancient city of Kámiros just a little way inland. **Kámiros** is the most complete of the ancient sites on Rhodes, despite being the smallest of the three cities, and it brings to life the daily routine of the ordinary people of the Hellenistic era. The earliest relics found here date back to Mycenaean times but it became a major settlement in post Minoan times after 1500 BC, when a population of Cretans fled their devastated homeland and settled here. The ruins that we see today date mainly from post 226 BC, as buildings from the earlier era were destroyed by a powerful earthquake in that year.

The remains climb the hillside in clear urban zones typical of the time. As you enter the site you find yourself at the

Agora Square – meeting place of the people and flanked by several temples. Climb the steps ahead of you and turn right to walk up along the main street trodden by so many ancient sandals, and examine row upon row of small square rooms to your right and left; each was a family home. This residential area linked the lower social area with the religious sanctuary above. Climb up the steps to find a wall of stone ahead of you. These are the remains of what was a fantastic *stoa* (covered walkway) 200 m (660 ft) in length, built in the 3rd century BC. It must have been extremely impressive in its time, with shops at the rear and an open front supported by a series of double Doric columns, allowing the citizens – and today's visitors – to survey the whole city below them as they went about their business. Behind the wall at its northern end is a huge **cistern** dating from the 6th century BC. Until the *stoa* was built, this cistern stored the city's water (600 cubic metres when full), which was then supplied by a sophisticated system of pipes down through the development below. Climb above the cistern to the Acropolis and the remains of the sacred precinct of the **Temple of Athena**, once the crowning glory of the city. The rise of Rhodes Town brought about the gradual decline of Kámiros. Luckily for

Explore the Hellenic ruins of ancient Kámiros, standing for more than a millenium.

modern visitors the city was not seen as a great prize to be plundered, rather it was simply abandoned when it outlived its usefulness, leaving us with a rich legacy of urban detail. However, there is still a vast amount hidden under the soil of the surrounding area with tales yet untold.

There are several fish tavernas along the coastline near Ancient Kámiros. Some cater to the tour bus crowd and can be busy at lunchtime. For an even prettier spot head 15 km (9 miles) further south to **Kámiros Skála** (Kámiros Harbour), with its tiny fishing fleet. You'll be able to watch the comings and goings of the daily *caïque* to the island of Chálki just off the coast – there is a daily roundtrip service all year round.

As the road climbs away from Kámiros Skála, the ruined castle of Kritinia (sometimes called Kastéllos) comes into view on your right. This site is one of the delights of southern Rhodes because, as yet, it is not on the tour company itinerary and you will only share it with a few other people. As you approach the castle look for a large Greek flag that has the initial impression of being a ticket office. An enterprising lady has set out her fruit stall here, and, before you know it, you'll be taking home piles of grapes or melons. Buy if you want but she is not an official guardian of the castle and there is no fee to enter, so don't feel guilty about declining her offer.

Kritiniá Castle was built by the knights in the 16th century as one of a series of strongholds to protect this western coastline. Smaller than the main castles it has a keep built around the rocky summit with a lookout tower and a simple vaulted chapel. A population of 'Rhodes dragons' – lizards with frilled necks – scurry along the walls and disappear between cracks in the rocks. Make sure that you are as sure-footed, since there are no rails or barriers here and the drops can be hair-raising.

*A bevy of scurrying lizards are the only residents
left at the ruins of Kritiniá Castle.*

Kritiniá village sits a little way inland from the castle. Its whitewashed houses have a look of the Cycladic settlements on islands further north and there is a 12th-century church, **Áyios Ioánnis Pródhromos**, in the central square that displays frescoes from the 13th century. From here it is possible to head inland to the slopes of Mount Attávyros, at 1215 m (3986 ft), the highest peak on the island, and to the village of **Émbonas**, centre of Rhodian winemaking, which rests in its lea. During the grape harvest in late September, the air in the region takes on a sugary, fruity perfume as the grapes begin to give up their juice. In the centre of the village the CAIR and Emery wine factories both make extremely palatable wine and offer several tastings. You can visit between the hours of 9am–4.30pm in summer, 9am–3.30pm in winter. Try to visit early or late when there are no tour groups. Following this take a stroll up into the village with its pretty houses bedecked with bougainvillea. There are several tavernas lining the main street, along with stores selling locally made handcrafts and other items.

Émbonas also forms a starting point for hikes up to **Mount Attávyros** to the south. This barren treeless hump could not be more of a contrast to Profítis Ilías just a little way north. The roundtrip takes about seven hours but you will be rewarded with magnificent views as far as Crete on a clear day. There are also remains of a **temple to Zeus** built by the Mycenaeans.

Continuing south from Kritiniá the road climbs away from the coast through some pretty mountain scenery. A narrow single lane road leads through the village of **Siána**, and it is worth making a stop here because this is the only village on the island that is allowed to sell *soúma*, a distillation of the grape skins made after their juice has been taken for wine. The result is a strong concoction similar to *schnapps* and it is sold in unlabelled bottles at the roadside. If *soúma* doesn't sound like your cup of tea, you could buy excellent honey and yogurt, or finely crafted woollen rugs and throws cleverly displayed against the whitewashed

In Émbonas village, grapes are harvested and collected for Rhodian winemaking.

Barely visible amidst the rocks is the Castle of Monólithos – or, at least, what is left of it.

walls to enhance the colours and patterns. Before leaving take a look at the clock on the church tower. The hands and face have been painted on – so time really does stand still here.

Eventually the road leads to **Monólithos**, a rural village noted for its artisans. The reason for visiting Monólithos lies 2 km (1 mile) beyond the modern houses. The remains of a knight's castle sits atop an impressive rocky pinnacle 250 m (800 ft) above the surrounding coastal plain – hence the name; Monólithos means 'one rock'. Views as you approach by road are great photographic opportunities and from there it is difficult to see how you could possibly climb to the summit. Inside the walls, there is little left of the other castle structures but a tiny whitewashed chapel adds a typical Greek touch to the image. Enjoy the views out towards Chálki, and the silence, punctuated only by birdsong and the sound of the sea breezes.

South of Monólithos the road is only gradually being improved and it leads around to the village of **Kattaviá** for access to the Prasonísi peninsula.

EXCURSIONS

As part of a greater island group, the Dodecanese, Rhodes offers the opportunity to visit several neighbours – each on a day trip. You can also take a trip to a different country – Turkey – lying just off the island's east coast.

Kos

A two-and-a-half hour hydrofoil trip from Rhodes, Kos is the second most populated island in the Dodecanese and has seen human settlement since ancient times. With safe harbours and wide fertile plains, it could both protect and feed its people. It is also one of the most popular islands with package holiday-makers, although its many fine attractions can be offset by young Europeans indulging in high-spirited behaviour. Try to

> **Good morning – kaliméra.**
> **Good evening – kalispéra.**
> **Good night – kaliníchta.**

visit early or late in the season to avoid their worst excesses. **Kos Town** on the western coast is the main settlement, and is a fascinating place to explore. Settled for many centuries, it suffered an earthquake in 1933 which damaged much of the modern town centre but allowed Italian archaeologists to excavate a large section of the **Roman city** directly underneath. Today it is possible to walk through the old Agora and along Roman roads at the western section of the town, which sit side-by-side with 21st century thoroughfares and shopping streets.

Later, following the fall of Jerusalem after the unsuccessful final crusade, the town became a stronghold of the Knights of St John and in the 15th century they built a large castle, **The Castle of the Knights of St John**, at the water's edge. It still forms an impressive backdrop for photographs of **Mandráki Harbour**, and is filled with historical 'litter' that includes carved marble plaques, statuary and cannons.

Ottoman forces ousted the knights in 1522, and evidence of their stay can be found just inland from the castle. The minaret of the **Loggia Mosque**, built in the 18th century and the largest on Kos, now stands silent and closed but it is matched by a number of smaller examples throughout the town – some are still in use by the small Muslim population.

Beside the mosque – in fact almost overshadowing it – is a large plane tree. Its branches extend so far that it has had to be supported for many years by a framework of scaffolding. The local people will tell you that this is the **Hippocrates Tree**, under which the 'father of medicine,' a native of the island, would lecture to his students over 2,500 years ago. Sadly, although the tree has been proven to be one of the oldest in Europe, most experts believe that it is only 2,000 years old and therefore not of Hippocrates' era, although you'll see a bronze statue of this most famous son along the harbourfront.

In the main square of the town (walk inland from the mosque on the south side of the Agora to find it) is the

The sunset over the west coast islands is a sublime vision, paralleled by few natural sights in all of Greece.

Archaeological Museum, which features finds from ancient Kos including mosaics and domestic utensils found by the Italian team. On the outskirts of the town, on E Grigorou Street, is a small **Roman Odeon** or theatre, used in summer for performances. Nearby is **Casa Romana** (currently closed pending renovations), a Roman villa recreated in detail to bring to life the daily routine of a wealthy Roman family.

If you don't want to walk around town, a small motorised train, which operates several times a day during the summer, runs past all all the major sites.

Four km (2.5 miles) out of Kos Town are the remains of the medical school founded in the 4th century BC, in the years after the death of Hippocrates. The **Asclepium** was a major centre of healing and also offered spa facilities using the mineral-rich water supplies. Many of the largest remains date from the Roman, rather than Classical Greek era, and the site was damaged by the Knights of St John when they removed marble to build their castle in Kos town. The main Doric temple rested on the upper level of the three terraces that make up the site. There are fine views across to Turkey from here.

Chálki

The largest of a group of islands lying just 10 miles off the west coast of Rhodes, Chálki could not be more of a contrast to its larger sibling. It relies on Rhodes for its water supply and consequently the natural population and visitor numbers have to be kept low – maintaining the unspoiled atmosphere.

The residents of Chálki made a decent living from sponge diving, until the animals died out in the early 20th century. At that time, there was a mass emigration to Florida, where natives of Chálki and other Greek islands founded the settlement of Tarpon Springs and carried on their traditional trade. These expats later sent money to the remaining

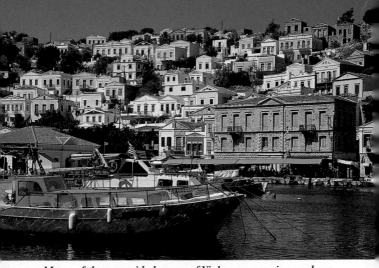

Many of the quayside houses of Yialos are pensions, where visitors to the island of Symi can take a room for the night.

population that funded the building of the first highway on the island.

Boats dock at the main settlement of **Emboriós**, where streets of Neo-Classical mansions are crowned by the elegant campanile of the church of **Áyios Nikólaos**. You'll find a number of eateries here for a leisurely lunch. Inland from Emboriós is the old capital of **Chorió** – now deserted save for 15 August when the festival of the Assumption is celebrated at the **Church of the Panagía**. The single road leads from Emboriós past the sandy bay of Pontamo to Chorio, but otherwise Chálki is a place for walking, where you are free to explore the landscape and breathe the fresh air. The most popular excursion leads to the **Monastery of Áyios Ioánnis Pródhrómos**.

Symi

Barren Symi is a tiny island, yet 100 years ago it was one of the wealthiest in the Aegean. Shipbuilding was its major industry, along with maritime trading and sponge diving. Shipyard owners, captains, and tradesmen built fine mansions and ornate churches, giving the island the epithet 'jewel of the Dodecanese'; however, when powered ships became the vogue this coincided with a change in trading conditions and a blight on the sponge crop. Symi's production dropped, and soon most of the workforce emigrated to the US and Australia. Symi's buildings were left to fall into a gradual decline, and its streets fell silent. However, in the 1970s and '80s it was rediscovered by the Greek avant-garde, who fell in love with its mansions and other decaying buildings, feeling that they were ideal for second homes.

Today, many have been restored and arrival at Symi's major port **Yialós** offers one of the most impressive vistas in Greece. Hundreds of Neo-Classical stone façades intermingled with thousands of pastel-painted balconies, windows and shutters rise from the harbourside and over the nearby hills.

The small permanent population is joined by a number of holidaymakers in the summer, although there are no large hotels on the island and accommodation is generally found in small pensions, private rooms or studios. By far the greatest number of people visit Symi on a day trip from Rhodes, about 1 hour and 30 minutes away. Visitors disembark from ships around 10.30am and depart at 4pm. Consequently, the island has two distinct moods – a daytime bustle and relaxed languor in the late afternoons and evening.

Yialós was always the commercial heart of the island, and if you walk along the seafront you'll find yourself tempted by vendors selling natural sponges, spices and olive oil soap.

The Sponge Centre not only sells sponges, it explains in detail the lifecycle of this strange creature, which until recent years was thought to be a plant rather than an animal. Restaurants along the seafront entice you to stop for a delicious seafood meal, but there is still more to see.

High above Yialós, hidden from sight by several hills is **Chóra**, the old capital of the island, reached by a whitewashed route of 357 steps, the **Kalí Stráta**, or 'good steps'– or by taxi if you don't feel

> **Dress appropriately for church and monastery visits.**

you have the energy. Here, the fast pace of life at the port gives way to a more traditional speed. Older people sit in shady doorways and sleeping cats seem oblivious to passing feet. Chóra is crowned by an impressive Byzantine fortress, the **Kástro**, where the **Panagía** (Church of the Virgin Mary), has extremely impressive frescoes. The town also has a small archaeological museum.

The island has another 76 churches, many of which can be reached on foot. Most day trips from Rhodes will allow you to visit the **Panormítis Monastery** in the south of the island as part of your itinerary; unfortunately you will find yourself surrounded by people from several other boats who arrive at exactly the same time. At the heart of this small compound is a 16th-century church, the Taxiarchis Michail (Archangel Michael) of Panormítis, with richly jewelled icons of St Michael and Archangel Gabriel.

Marmaris

Though protracted conflict between Greece and Turkey carried on well into the 20th century, the two communities seem to be

The clock tower of the Panormítis Monastery on Symi stands like a beacon over the tiny island.

Stretch out the parameters of your holiday and take a trip to Turkey for the day.

putting the past behind them. Many Greek islands sit close to the mainland Turkish coast, and it is now possible to take advantage of sea crossings and enjoy a day trip to this totally different – yet strangely similar – country.

From Rhodes, the nearest Turkish town is Marmaris, just over an hour away by hydrofoil or catamaran. You'll need to take your passport, for customs control, and some foreign currency. Although Turkey uses the Turkish Lira – needed for small transactions – you'll probably find that for many purchases sterling, US dollars or euros are more welcomed by vendors to counter constant devaluations in the value of the domestic currency.

Marmaris is set on a wide shallow bay backed by a range of fragrant pine-clad hills that shelter it from the southerly breezes – consequently, it is much hotter in the summer than Rhodes.

The resort of Marmaris, one of the largest in Turkey, has grown rapidly along the bayside with a rash of concrete hotels set behind the sandy beach. Alhough the new parts of town are not especially pretty, the old town is like a small pearl in the centre of it all. Eminently walkable, it lures visitors to its labyrinth of small alleyways and shady squares.

Sitting atop the small knoll around which the old town is built is **Marmaris castle** (Müze), offering wonderful views across the bay and the pretty waterfront below. To reach the castle entrance you'll need to negotiate your way through the **souk**, or bazaar – numerous shaded streets selling bargains galore at prices much cheaper than in Rhodes. Carpets are the major item here, and there are several major suppliers in town.

Turkish markets have long been famed for the range of goods – from leather and spices to gold; however, overall there is not as much choice as in Rhodes Old Town. The most popular items are copies of designer labels, but the finish and quality of many goods is low. The atmosphere is also much more frenetic, with stallholders coming out to shake you by the hand and entice you to look at their wares. You are sure to be offered a Turkish apple tea if you are serious about buying. A sense of humour is essential if you are only browsing, as the sales pitch is more concerted than in Greece. One 'value-for-money' service offered in Marmaris is the shoe shine. For a few Turkish Lira you'll get an excellent finish courtesy of a genial man who mixes exactly the right polish from the numerous brass containers at his stand.

Useful Expressions in Turkish

Good morning/ afternoon.	**Iyi günler.**	iyi gunlèr
Goodbye.	**Allahaısmar- ladık/Güle güle.**	âllââ'aısmâr- lâdık/gulè gulè
Please ...	**Lütfen ...**	lutfeun
Thank you.	**Teşekkür ederim.**	tèchèkkur èdèrim
Yes/No	**Evet/Hayır.**	èvèt/'âïïr
Excuse me.	**Affedersiniz.**	âffèdèrsiniz

Following a few hours of bargain-hunting, head down to the waterside for a refreshing drink and perhaps lunch. There are numerous eateries along the water's edge and you can watch the distinctive wooden *gulet* tour boats coming and going. You may be surprised to find that many of the items on the menu are the same as on Rhodes – only the name changes. This is because these two communities have lived closely together, though not always happily, for several hundred years.

One very recent development in Marmaris is the **Netsel Marina**, with berths for over 800 sailboats. It is one of the favourite destinations for sailors who ply the Turkish coast in the summer, being well stocked with shops and other facilities and only a couple of minutes' stroll to the old town.

These wooden Turkish tourboats – gulets – are moored in a neat line along the quayside in Marmaris.

Highlights

Rhodes Old Town. Medieval citadel built by the Knights of the Order of St John with original buildings and streets. Later remains from the Ottoman period 16th–20th century. Tax-free port. Free.

Grand Masters Palace. Odós Ippotón, Rhodes Old Town; Tel: 2241 023 359. Renovated Palace of the Grand Master of the Order of the Knights of St John with Hellensitic, Roman and early-Christian mosaics. Open Tues–Sun 8am–7pm. Entrance fee.

Odós Ippotón. Rhodes Old Town. Medieval street with Inns of the Order of the Knights of St John. Free.

Archaeology Museum. Platía Mousiou, Rhodes Old Town; Tel. 2241 027 657. Old Hospital of the knights housing ancient finds from Rhodes and neighbouring islands. Open Tues–Sat 8am–7pm, Sun 8.30am–3pm. Entrance fee

Sound and Light Show. Rimini Square, Rhodes New Town; Fun interpretation of historic of Rhodes events. Entrance fee.

Ialysós and Filérimos Monastery. Ialysós plateau; Tel. 2241 092 202. Remains of ancient city-state and medieval monastery. Open Tues–Sun 8am–7pm. Entrance fee.

Kamirós. Tel. 2241 040 037. Remains of Hellenistic city state. Open Tues–Sun 8am–7pm. Entrance fee.

Líndos. Beautiful village of traditional Rhodian homes and captains' houses. No telephone. Free.

Líndos Acropolis. Líndos; Tel. 2244 031 258. Sanctuary to Athena (6th century BC) and medieval citadel. Open Tues– Sun 8am–6.40pm, Mon 12.30pm–6.40pm. Entrance fee.

Petaloúdhes (Valley of the Butterflies). Wooded valley with cooling streams and population of rare moths. Open Tues–Sun 8am–6.40pm. Entrance fee.

Eptá Pigés (Seven Springs). Kolymbia. No phone. Woodland with lake and countryside walks. Free.

Symi Island. No telephone. Small island with pretty port of renovated Neo-Classical mansions and older inland Chora of traditional homes. Free entrance; fee for boat trip from Rhodes.

WHAT TO DO

Rhodes is not only an excellent holiday destination in terms of its many ancient sites, museums and historic attractions – it also offers a fabulous range of sporting, shopping and entertainment opportunities to the visitor.

Island hopping: Rhodes offers the perfect base for visiting several islands on a day trip. Kos is a busy island with the same kind of atmosphere as Rhodes, but other smaller islands such as Symi or Chálki offer a different, more relaxed, ambiance. Perhaps you want to visit a different country for the day – try a trip to Turkey for bargain-hunting in the old bazaar in the town.

You can book trips on commercial ferries from ticket agents near the main harbour. For nearby islands, smaller tour boats sell tickets from small desks on Mandráki harbour. Tour companies also offer trips, which include transfer to the boat and back to your hotel for a price premium.

BEACHES

For most people travelling to Rhodes, beach activities figure highly on their list of priorities. Beaches on the island come in all sizes, from the tiny cove where you can spend the day alone, to wide sandy bays where you can be sure of the company of hundreds. On Rhodes the beaches may comprise sand, pebbles or a mixture of the two.

Though many people prefer soft sand over the pebble beach, keep in mind that when the summer Meltemi winds blow across the Aegean and cool the west coast, pebbles of coin size won't blow around and spoil your day. Pebbles predominate on the coastline around Ixiá, although the beach of Rhodes Town itself is mostly sand. The best sandy beaches are along the more sheltered east coast – wide and sandy at Faliráki, and Kálathos, with wonderful small bays at Stegná, Agáthi and Líndos.

On most of these beaches topless sunbathing is accepted, but it is still frowned upon if you find yourself on a beach frequented by Greek families – such beaches usually have few amenities and are less of an obvious lure to tourists.

SPORTS

Watersports: You'll find a whole range of watersports available on Rhodes. Jet skis are popular almost everywhere; you can rent them by the half hour and head off into open water for a speed 'rush'. Many beaches also have water rides in which you can be pulled along on a raft behind a speed boat. Great fun for kids, but unnerving for watching parents. Try a pedalo if you want something a little more genteel.

Windsurfing is best where the prevailing wind and wide sandy bays allow the sail to catch the breezes; perfect conditions exist at Prasonísi in the far south, which acts as a magnet to serious surfers. Wind conditions are also good at Ixiá.

Diving and snorkelling: Although the warm clear waters of the Aegean are a perfect diving environment,

The winds along the west coast of the island are ideal for windsurfing.

the Greek government has been rightly concerned about the possible damage of submerged ancient sites and theft of important artifacts. However, diving is now a legal and welcomed activity, encouraged by the government, provided that you dive with an approved and registered organisation.

If you have never scuba-dived before, each dive centre is registered by the Greek government to offer training in addition to dive supervision for qualified divers. All centres are affiliated with one of the major certifying bodies – PADI (Professional Association of Diving Instructors) is the most common. The basic qualification, the Open Water certificate, takes five days to complete. On completion this will allow you to dive with an instructor to a depth of 18m (60 ft), which opens up many dive sites in the area around Rhodes to you.

Many centres also offer an introductory session, commonly known as the 'Discover Scuba Programme'. This involves a morning or afternoon of theory and shallow water work, giving you the chance to try out the basic techniques before you decide to do the full open-water course. Contact Dive Mediterranean Centre (DMC) Tel. (2241) 061 115; fax. (2241) 066 584 for details of the programmes available.

You can rent or buy snorkelling equipment in all the major resorts, allowing you to explore the beach shallows and hundreds of rocky inlets along the coastline. You'll see urchins, shoals of fish and even small octopuses that make their homes in rocky crevices just offshore.

Walking and Hiking: Exploring the coastline or interior of Rhodes offers a different experience at various times of year. In late spring the hillsides are awash with flowers, and crops of corn give the fields a golden hue. As summer progresses and the crops are harvested (usually early July), the ground dries and becomes more dusty. The distinctive chirrup of the cicada sounds through the heat of the day. In autumn the earth gives back the heat it absorbed during the summer, as the air begins to cool. Spring and fall offer the clearest air for panoramic views of the surrounding land; a heat haze rises in summer, cutting long-distance visibility.

Inland, you can walk to the summit of Mount Attávyros from Émbonas, to the summit of Profítis Ilías from Apollona, and around the village of Láerma in central south Rhodes, for wonderful images of country life. The coastal walk from Kallitheá to Líndos – especially from Tsambíka to Líndos – offers some spectacular views and photo opportunities. Or head across to Chálki or Symi islands, where there are few people and even fewer vehicles.

Don't forget to take a supply of water and wear sturdy footwear. If you want to walk in summer, early mornings or late afternoons are the best times of day to go.

SHOPPING

The weaving maze of small streets that make up the old towns of Rhodes and Líndos are home to a fascinating mixture of art and sculpture galleries, jewellers, clothing boutiques, 'collectable' and kitsch stores. Shopping is one of the great delights of a trip to Rhodes, and it is possible to spend hours browsing for the perfect

The Turkish Quarter is the place to go when shopping for souvenirs from Rhodes.

souvenir. The Old Town still maintains some of the atmosphere of its old Ottoman bazaar.

Rhodes Town is also a duty-free port, and this means that prices on items such as cameras, watches and jewellery will be 15 percent cheaper than in the rest of Europe – maybe even more. You'll see numerous, fine, air-conditioned, boutiques selling the best-known brand names and, early or late in the season, you may be able to barter for an even greater price reduction.

Antiques: For serious collectors there are genuine antiques (anything made or produced before 1821 is officially classified as an antique). These could be in the form of sculpture, pottery or icons. They will require proper accreditation and, in some cases, a permit if they are to be exported from the country – the antiques dealer should be able to advise you

in this process. For those whose budget or expertise won't stretch to the real thing, you will be able to buy reproductions of these same articles, at varying quality and a range of prices.

Ceramics and Sculpture: Rhodes still has a thriving ceramics industry in villages such as Archángelos, where you will find roadside workshops and retail stores. Plates, jugs and

At every turn, vendors will have a variety of lace and embroidered pieces.

bowls are produced in a bewildering number of patterns and colours. Popular traditional themes are copies of the Minoan patterns from Crete, or pottery with scenes taken from ancient Greek frescoes or mosaics. At the bottom end of the market, try fridge magnets in the shape of Ionian or Corinthian columns.

Copies of Classical pieces are also popular. Prices can vary enormously due to huge differences in the quality of the materials used and the skills of the workman involved. You will soon be able to discern this after visiting a few different stores and closely examining the products.

> Siesta time is observed between 3pm and 5pm. Be quiet in villages at this time.

Look out for the weight of a piece of pottery or sculpture and the detail in the decoration or the carving.

Brass and Copperware: Brass and copper have traditionally been used in homes and on farms because they are hard-wearing. Today, as younger members of society turn their backs on the rural ways of life, many of these items are finding their way to dealers in the Old Town. Tureens, jugs, bowls and coffeepots are just some of the items – many come from the Turkish era of Rhodes history.

Clothing: Traditional Greek clothing is hard to come by, but Rhodes Town and Líndos have narrow lanes festooned with cool cotton or cheesecloth trousers, tops and dresses that are ideal for the summer climate. You will also find the ubiquitous T-shirt in a variety of styles, along with swimwear and footwear.

Both towns have a plethora of choices of designer clothing, but there is a thriving market in copies of the latest street names for a fraction of the cost. Quality may not be the same as the genuine article, but you must judge that for yourself.

Leather and Fur: The islanders have always worked the leather from their arable herds and make handbags, purses, belts and footwear in a variety of styles and patterns. You will also find boutiques in Rhodes Old Town selling the very best in high-quality fur and leather coats or jackets. Pelts are

The Genuine Icon

Icon is the word used to describe a religious portrait, usually of a saint or apostle. They are symbolic of the persona and were a development from the *fayum* paintings that covered the face of the dead in the sarcophagi of Egyptian mummies.

Icons lie at the heart of Byzantine or Orthodox worship and they form a focus for prayer. Some are said to possess miraculous healing powers or the ability to perform miracles, although in church, all are considered holy. The characteristic gold leaf used in their production symbolised the glory of God. The earliest examples date from the later part of the first millennium.

Icon painters created works for churches but also for private clients, and for centuries they were popular souvenirs of the grand European Tour or religious pilgrimage. However, modern production methods, including thin artificial canvas and gaudy synthetic colours, saw them lose favour.

In recent years there has been a rebirth in icon painting using traditional methods, both for church renovations and for commercial sale. Natural pigments and egg tempura (egg yolk and vinegar) binding are painstakingly mixed and applied to a canvas bound over wood. The gold leaf is then applied, and the whole image is given a patina. This time-consuming work is exquisite and correspondingly expensive.

imported with few restrictions and made-to-measure items can be produced in just a few days.

Carpets: A few shops in the Old Town still produce and sell 'Turkish' carpets. You'll see ladies working at the complicated patterns on looms in the doorways and the carpets hung enticingly on the walls to tempt you to stop and look. Traditional 'Greek' carpets woven on smaller looms are still produced in villages such as Archángelos, on Rhodes. These are of a coarser texture than those made in Turkey and are traditionally decorated with motifs such as dolphins or deer framed by a geometric pattern.

An assortment of gold and silver jewellery is sold at bargain prices in Rhodes.

Jewellery: Precious stones glitter in shops, and you can feel free to choose as many carats as your budget can handle. Gold and silver are sold by weight, with relatively little extra cost added for personal workmanship, which makes them a good buy. Ancient Greek designs are very much in evidence in gold, silver and non-precious metals. Favourite designs are Hellenic, Minoan and Macedonian.

At the other price extreme there are many forms of everyday jewellery – ankle chains in metal or leather, navel studs, and finger and toe rings.

A guitarist and bouzouki player fill a Greek taverna with traditional music.

Edible delicacies: The abundant fruit grown on the islands in the summer has always been preserved to last through the cold winters. Cherries, plums, figs and other fruits are made into jams. Bees harvest the pollen of the wild herbs on the hillsides to produce delicious honey to which fresh almonds or walnuts are added. Olives are preserved either in oil or brine, or simply take home 'extra virgin cold pressed' (the first pressing) oil both for cooking and delicious salad dressings.

Rhodes also does a thriving trade in low-cost liquor, and many of the ancient stone storage warehouses of the Old Town now house huge stocks of the international brands of whisky, cognac and other alcoholic concoctions. If you want to take a Greek drink home with you then try *oúzo* – the best is said to come from the island of Lesvos.

ENTERTAINMENT

Sound and Light Shows: One of the most exciting and mystical ways to view the Old Town is during a Sound and Light Show, held nightly in summer. There is a seating area reached from Rimini Square, which lies on the old moat area to the west of the town. The evocative story of the history of the great battle against Suleiman unfolds as lights play on the warm sandstone walls – an absolute must on any trip to the island (Tel. 0241 21922).

Music and Dance: For many, the image of Greek music and dance is inexorably linked to the film *Zorba the Greek*. Anthony Quinn performs the *syrtaki* dance (in fact an amalgam of several different traditional dances), to the sound of the *bouzouki*, a stringed guitar-type instrument that

> Open – anichtó
> Closed – klistó

produces melodic, slightly metallic sounds. When played live, it has a haunting melody, but taverna owners do have the irritating habit of playing it at high decibels through over-loaded speakers. This does a great disservice to the Greek musical tradition, which is rich, varied and goes back hundreds of years. Musical rhythms were traditionally matched to the complex cadences of the epic poetry of Greece. These are very different from the 'four beats to a bar' that characterise the western musical tradition and therefore it is sometimes difficult to follow. Each region of Greece has its own particular songs and dances. The music of the southern islands has a traditional style called *nisiótika*, and the *syrtós* dance (steps performed in a circle) is a universal element in Greek dance.

It is becoming more difficult to see genuine performances. Cultural festivals are one opportunity, but the better way is at a private wedding or feast day when the performances are set in their true context (see Calendar of Events on page 92). Luckily Rhodes benefits from having the Nelly Dimoglou dance troupe. This company is dedicated to preserving the traditional dances from each region of Greece. They perform nightly throughout the tourist season at the Traditional Dance Centre on Odós Androníkou in the Old Town. For information, Tel. 2241 020 157. If you cannot get to see a performance, most large hotels will hold a 'Greek night' once each week, with music and dancing. While not necessarily completely authentic, they do allow you to get a feel for the passion and movement in Greek dance, and to get into the swing of things by joining in yourself.

Clubbing and gambling: For those who can't go on holiday without the hope of throbbing music into the early hours of the morning, look no further than Faliráki and Líndos. After dark, these resorts throb with the latest sounds until the sun comes up. During July and August the antics of young Europeans out for a good time can become rather raucous, and these resorts draw hedonistic pleasure-seekers like a magnet. Follow the crowds to the latest hotspot, which changes almost every year.

If you enjoy the excitement of the wheels, tables and cards, the Playboy Casino on Aktí Miaoúli in the New Town is open nightly during the tourist season, and is a fun way of playing with chance and perhaps mixing with some high rollers.

THINGS TO DO FOR CHILDREN

Rhodes is a great place to take children. Greek society is very family oriented, and children will be pampered and indulged in cafés and restaurants. Most resort hotels have a range of activities specially designed for children, including kids' clubs, designated swimming areas and playgrounds.

Since the Mediterranean has little tidal range and offers many wide shallow bays, there are many places that are safe for paddling and swimming for children. Sandy beaches are more fun than pebbly ones for castle-building and hole-digging, so bear that in mind when choosing your accommodation. Do remember when taking young children to the beach that the sun can be extremely hot. Keep young skin safe by covering with cream or a T-shirt, even when in the water.

For older children, the range of watersports found in the popular resorts offers an exciting challenge. From pedalos and canoes to wind-surfing and jet-skiing – the choice is yours. For those who prefer water without sand, try the water park at Faliráki, complete with slides – and fun for all ages.

Older children may also want to try the 'death-defying' bungy jumps, 'sling-shot' rides and the carting track found at Faliráki. These are certainly not for the faint-hearted.

What child could resist a ride up the hillside of Líndos on an adorable little donkey?

The trip to the cooling woodland of Petaloúdhes or 'butterfly valley' to search for moths is a great adventure for the budding naturalist. The kids will love riding on a donkey from Líndos to the Acropolis or, for more animals, you can visit the ostrich farm near the valley of the butterflies.

Caïque trips – these small prettily painted boats ply their routes from the main resorts to nearby beaches. Children love to watch the coastline go by, or point out shoals of small fish swimming in the clear water.

Calendar of Events

1 January: Called Protochroniá, but also St Basil's Day, when sprigs of basil are given as traditional gifts. Card games on Rhodes set luck for the coming year.

6 January: Epiphany, when young men dive into the cold water to recover a crucifix. Those who do are considered blessed for the year.

7 March: Union of the Dodecanese with Greece – parades and folk dancing.

26 March: Greek Independence Day, military parades.

Clean Monday: First day of Lent marked by frugal meals – house cleaning and laundry are undertaken with enthusiasm.

Easter: This is the most important of the Orthodox holidays. Candlelit processions follow a flower-decked bier on Good Friday. On Holy Saturday a sacred flame is passed to each household that lights a lamp of faith. On Sunday lambs are sacrificed and roasted, signifying the beginning of another Spring.

23 April: St George's Day – the patron saint of Greece.

1 May: May Day, marked by processions and flower festivals.

Pentacost: Festival at St Michael's Monastery at Panormítis.

24 June: Birthday of St John the Baptist – feasts and bonfires.

15 August: Assumption Day. Processions and festivals across the island.

August/September: Cultural festivals at Maritsá, Kalythiés and Émbonas.

8 September: Day of pilgrimage to Tsambíka Monastery and festival at Moni Skiádi near Messanagrós, both in honour of the Virgin Mary.

26 October: Wine-tasting festival at Émbonas.

28 October: National Ochi (No) Day, commemorating Greek defiance of the Italian invasion of 1940.

December: Carolling in the days before Christmas and on New Year's Eve.

EATING OUT

Greek cuisine makes no pretense of emulating the classic cuisine of countries such as France, but it has always used local and seasonal ingredients at their peak of flavour and freshness, cooked in the simplest of fashions – on a grill, or slowly in the oven. The people have relied on staples such as olive oil, wild herbs, seafood, lamb or goat meat and an abundance of fresh vegetables, fruit and nuts since the islands were settled several millennia ago. Today, the Greek diet is considered one of the healthiest in the world, and its population is one of the longest living. The extensive use of vegetables makes eating out a delight for non-meat eaters.

Where to eat

Greece has a fascinating range of eateries, which at first glance can, be a little confusing for the visitor. However, once you realise that Greek families traditionally never ate a three-course meal in one establishment, it brings the whole picture together. The appetiser and main course were eaten in one establishment. The family then moved on to another place for sweets, and yet another place for coffee. As tourist numbers grow, this system is breaking down, and many on Rhodes are changing to the European or American standard.

The *ouzerí* is a traditional establishment selling not only the fiery but pleasant alcoholic drink, but also the *mezédhes* dishes that accompany it – *oúzo* is never drunk on an empty stomach. These can simply be a couple of appetisers or a full meal of several different small dishes. All will be absolutely fresh and delicious. Octopus or squid is traditionally served with *oúzo* but it is not compulsory; you will also have a range of hot and cold vegetable and meat dishes to choose from.

You're sure to find something to suit your pleasure in the many shops and cafés along the main street of Faliráki.

Visit the *psistariá* – the gyro and souvlaki shop. This most ancient of fast foods makes a tasty lunch or snack. Later peruse the amazing choice at the *zacharoplastío* (pastry shop) or the *galaktopolío*, which specialises in yogurt, cheese and other dairy dishes.

The *kafenío* is the Greek coffee shop, traditionally the domain of the male, and still so in the inland villages. Usually very plainly decorated, with a few old tables and chairs outside, it is the focus of heated political debate and serious backgammon games.

However, it is the *tavérna* (you'll find it spelled *tabepna* on many Greek signs because *b* is pronounced *v* and *p* is pronounced *r* in the Greek language) that is at the heart of

Greek hospitality, and where the appetiser and *entrée* courses have always been taken.

Many restaurants on Rhodes offer bland versions of authentic Greek dishes or a series of Euro dishes for a tourist palate. Our advice to find authentic cuisine is to follow the local people. You may find yourself in some backstreet eatery away from the pretty views, but you can be sure that the food is excellent.

When to eat

Many tavernas in the major resorts will be open to serve breakfast, lunch and dinner (many offer a cooked English breakfast). Traditionally, breakfast has been a small meal for Greeks – they basically enjoy a Continental breakfast of bread, jam or honey, and coffee. Lunch is eaten at around 3pm, followed by a siesta, before work begins

> **Salt and pepper can be in confusing pots – one hole for pepper, many holes for salt.**

again at around 5.30pm. Dinner is taken late – usually around 10pm, and in summer tavernas will serve food as late as 1am.

Conversely, if you want to eat early, most tavernas will begin their evening service at around 6pm. You will definitely have your choice of tables if you eat before 7.30pm, but restaurants will lack the colourful atmosphere of the later evening when local people come out to eat.

The Menu

In the majority of traditional restaurants you will be presented with an extensive menu list, but not everything on it is available, as many foods are seasonal or made in batches (such as *mousakás*). Items currently available will have a price beside them.

Some of the best and most authentic restaurants in Greece will not even have a menu. The cook will prepare whatever is in season, and only a couple of dishes, to ensure that they are perfect. You simply go into the kitchen or to the grill to see what looks and smells most enticing, then make your choice.

All restaurants will render a cover charge. This charge includes a serving of bread and is usually no more than €0.80 per person.

Appetizers

Greece is one country where appetisers can constitute a full meal. *Mezédhes* (a selection of small appetiser dishes) shared by the whole table, offer a fun and relaxing way to eat – you simply have as little or as much as you want and keep ordering until you have had your fill, and restaurants have no qualms about taking orders for meals of 'appetisers only'. The most popular *mezédhes* are: *tzatzíki*, a yoghurt dip flavoured with garlic, cucumber and mint; *dolmádhes*, vine leaves stuffed with rice and vegetables, served both hot and cold; olives; *taramás*, cod-roe paste blended with breadcrumbs, olive oil and lemon juice; *gígantes,* large beans in tomato sauce; *kalamarákia tiganitá*, small pieces of deep-fried squid; *tiropitikia*, little pastry parcels filled with cheese; *pastourmás,* a kind of garlic sausage made with mutton or beef; and *keftedes*, meatballs flavoured with coriander and spices. *Saganáki* is a slice of feta cheese coated in breadcrumbs and then fried, but you can also have feta wrapped in foil with garlic and herbs and then cooked in the oven.

Greek salad or *horiátiki* (literally translated as 'village salad') of tomato, cucumber, onion and olives topped with feta cheese can be taken as a meal in itself. When adding

Greek food is one of the healthiest cuisines in the world – it incorporates lovely fresh seasonal ingredients.

salad dressing (bottles of olive oil and wine vinegar are found with other condiments on the table), always add vinegar to the salad first followed by oil. This is done to taste.

Soups are a staple of the diet in winter but availability is more limited in summer. Fish soup is a standard on many menus. *Avgolémono*, chicken broth with egg, lemon and rice, although delicious, is now fairly rare. *Mayirítsa*, made with lamb tripe, egg, lemon and lettuce, is a traditional Easter soup, which breaks the fasting of Lent.

Fish

It's no surprise that for centuries, seafood has formed a major part of the islanders' diet. You will find the day's catch on ice outside a taverna and will be asked to make your choice; this will be weighed and priced before cooking. Today, seafood is always a relatively expensive option by Greek standards because of over-fishing in the surrounding seas. Most common are *barboúnia* (red mullet), *xifías* (swordfish) and *lithrini* (bream). Seafood is always best served simply – it is often excellent when served grilled, with fresh lemon. *Marídhes* (little fish or whitebait) are served fried. If you like seafood stewed, try octopus (*oktapódhi*) with white wine, potatoes and tomatoes; or *garídhes* (prawns) in white wine. You can also find seafood served with white wine sauce, or sauces mixed with feta cheese.

Meat

Fast food to eat on the run includes *gýros* (thin slices of meat cut from a spit and served with salad on pitta bread), or *sou-*

vláki (small chunks of meat on a skewer also known by the Turkish name *kebab*). More formal barbecued dishes may include whole chickens, sides of lamb and veal, or stuffed loin of pork, all cooked to melting perfection. *Brizóla* is a basic steak, but it may automatically come well done rather than rare. Roasted or barbecued lamb is the traditional Easter fare.

Souvláki is a favourite dish – slowly grilled meat is served with many side dishes.

The superb Greek slow-cooked oven dishes and stews are well worth trying. *Kléftiko* is braised lamb with tomatoes, while *stifádho* is braised beef with onions – each comes in a small earthenware pot that keeps the contents piping hot.

Greece's most famous dish is probably *mousakás* – successive layers of aubergine (eggplant) and minced lamb with onions, all topped with béchamel sauce. At its best it should be firm but succulent, and aromatic with herbs. The best restaurants will make a fresh batch daily, and once it's gone you have to wait until tomorrow. *Pastítsio* is another layered dish, this time of pasta, meat and tomato sauce. *Giouvétsi* is beef stewed with small lozenge-shaped pasta.

> **Service is relaxed in Greek tavernas – enjoy the occasion.**

For those who want a hot vegetarian dish, *yemitsá* are tomatoes, aubergine or bell peppers stuffed with a delicious rice-and-vegetable mixture, or oven-cooked vegetables in a tomato sauce.

Dessert

Most tavernas will bring a plate of fresh fruit as a finale to your meal. If you feel the need for something more substantial, the *zacharoplastío* is the place to go. Here you will find *baklavás*, honey-soaked flaky pastry with walnuts; *kataïfi*, shredded wheat filled with chopped almonds and honey; or *pitta me meli*, honey cake.

If what you prefer is dairy desserts, don't despair, as there is a real variety of sweet treats to sample in Rhodes. You should try delicious Greek yogurt with honey or fruit, or *galaktoboúreko*, custard pie. In Rhodes Town, the majority of both *zacharoplastía* and *galaktopolía* can be found around the New Market, several have seats overlooking the bobbing tour boats of Mandraki Harbour.

An open-air bar in the bustling Turkish Quarter.

Cheese

Cheese is generally made from ewe's or goat's milk. The best-known soft Greek cheese is *féta,* popping up in almost every Greek salad. *Kaséri,* a hard cheese, is best eaten fresh but can also be used grated, like parmesan, and in cooked dishes.

Drinks

Rhodes has produced wine since Classical times, and for centuries it was a major industry on the island. Today, although not the classic vintages of French quality, there are some excellent producers and a good range to choose from. Free tastings are held regularly at the CAIR cooperative on Kapodistrias Street in Rhodes Town, and the Emery winery in Émbonas.

The two most famous CAIR wines are the white Ílios (dry) and red Chevalier de Rhodes, both simple table wines. Superior wines bear the Moulin label. CAIR also produce a good, sweet Muscat de Rhodes and two sparkling wines, Brut and Demi-sec, both fermented by the *champenoise* method.

Cheers (when drinking) *yámas*

The other major wine producer is Emery, whose table wines are eminently drinkable. The dry Villaré, of which only 120,000 bottles are produced each year, is very popular among the island's residents. Cava Emery is a heady red, which has to be matured for many months in oak barrels. In quite a number of years, this wine is as well-rated as many Burgundies. Emery also produce several sparkling wines, among them *cuvée close* and limited quantities of the Grand Prix, an excellent *méthode champenoise* wine.

Another option is to order wine from the barrel. This basic 'village' wine – red/white/rosé – will be served young and cool. Greece also produces wine flavoured with resin, called *retsína* – particularly useful in ancient times to keep the wine fresh in the hot climate. Retsina goes well with the Greek diet, but it is an acquired taste.

Oúzo is another drink that suits the hot climate. Taken as an aperitif, either neat or with ice and water, the aniseed flavour seems to cool the blood. However, don't overdo it, as drinking *oúzo* to excess can spark a mighty hangover.

Those who prefer beer can find Amstel and Heineken, brewed under license on the Greek mainland. Mythos is a native hellenic beer with a very crisp taste.

In Rhodes most of the major international brands of liquor are imported and then sold at reduced prices. A bewildering range makes it difficult to choose what to have for an aperitif or digestif.

Non-alcoholic drinks

Greece has fallen in love with the café *frappé* – strong cold coffee served over ice – which is especially refreshing in the heat of the day. Hot coffee is made *ellinikós,* or Greek style (indistinguishable from Turkish coffee), which is freshly brewed in individual copper pots and served in small cups. It will automatically arrive *glykývastos* (very sweet) unless you order *métrios* (medium) or *skétos* (without sugar). Those who prefer instant coffee can order a drink known simply by its trade name – nescafé or *nes.*

Soda comes in all the international varieties, or try one of the most refreshing drinks available – mineral water from Crete or the Greek mainland. Aoli is the most widespread domestic sparkling brand.

Reading the menu

I'd like a/an/some…	The íthela...
Could we have a table?	Tha boroúsame na échoume éna trapézi?

plate	piáto
napkin	trapezomándilo
cutlery	maheropírouna
glass	potíri
one	éna/mía
two	dhío
three	tris/tría
four	tésera
tea	éna tsaï
wine	krasí
beer	bíra
(iced) water	(pagoméno) neró

coffee	éna kafé
milk	gála
fish	psári
fruit	froúta
meat	kréas
bread	psomí
sugar	záchari
salt	aláti
pepper	pipéri
honey	méli
rice	rýzi
salad	mía saláta
soup	mía soúpa
egg	avgó
cheese	tyrí
beef	vodinó
pork	hirinó
chicken	kotópoulo
goat	katsiki
prawns	garídha
octopus	oktapódhi
aubergine (eggplant)	melitzána
garlic	skórdho
olives	elyés
lamb	arní
roasted or grilled	psitó
butter	voútyro
chick peas	revíthya
ice cream	pagotó
sauce	sáltsa
grape	stafýlia
tomato	domáta
lemon	lemóni

HANDY TRAVEL TIPS

An A–Z Summary of Practical Information

A

ACCOMMODATION

Hotels. Hotels are divided into six classes – Luxury, A, B, C, D and E. Room rates for all categories other than luxury are set by the Greek government. The classes are dictated by the facilities at the hotel, not the quality of the rooms. This means that a class-C hotel room may be just as acceptable as a class-A hotel one, but will not have facilities such as a conference room or hairdresser. Most hotels in class C and above are clean and reasonably furnished.

Many hotels on the island have contracts with European Tour operators. This means that at peak times it may be difficult to find the type of accommodation that you want. If you intend to travel in July and August, always make a firm booking before you arrive to avoid disappointment. At the beginning and end of the season (April and October), it will be possible to get a good deal as the island quiets down. Most hotels close from November to March. You will also find boarding houses or pensions, which come in three categories.

If you travel in peak season there may be a surcharge if you wish to book for less than three days. Local and national tax (around 4% and 8% respectively, plus a service charge of around 12%) will be added to the posted price.

If you need advice, the South Aegean Region Tourism Directorate for the Dodecanese (formerly the EOT) can help with reservations.

Private Accommodation. You will almost always be able to get some kind of accommodation in peak season, as many families have rooms or studios that they rent to visitors. All accommodation meeting an approved standard is given a special sign by the Tourism Directorate. If you arrive by ferry there will be someone at the port with photographs to show you their accommodation. It helps to know the geography of the island, as some private rooms/studios can be a distance away from the main towns or resorts. Have a map ready so that the room owner can point to exactly where it is.

Rhodes

I'd like a single/double room.   **Tha íthela éna monó/dipló domátio**
with bath/shower   **me bánio/dous**

AIRPORTS

Rhodes' Paradísi Airport is located on the west coast of the island 13 km (8 miles) south of Rhodes Town. For information, Tel. 2241 088 700.

From 6am–10.30pm there is a local bus connection into town; the bus leaves from outside the airport on the main road.

B

BICYCLE RENTAL

With no huge mountain ranges and relatively short distances between major attractions, Rhodes is a great place to tour by bike if you are fit. For many resorts it's a great way to get around. In Rhodes Town, The Bicycle Centre rents bikes and accessories. You can find them on Odós Gríva (Tel. 2241 028 315).

If you want information about organised cycling before you travel, contact the Greek Cycling Federation, 28 Odós Bouboulínas, 11 742 Athens; Tel. 2108 881 414.

BUDGETING FOR YOUR TRIP

Greece is a moderately inexpensive destination by European standards, with many price levels under government control. Here are some approximate prices to help you plan your budget, though these are subject to change.

One-way scheduled flight Athens to Rhodes: €90.

Boat ticket from Athens: €27 for a one-way ticket.

Price of one night for two in a mid-range hotel: €75–100.

Dinner in mid-range restaurant: €16–25.

Admission to museum/archaeological site: €3–6.

Car rental: €50 per day (for a small car in peak season).

Bus fare: ticket prices range from €1.50–€6. Rhodes to Líndos trips cost around €3.20.

Taxi fare airport–Rhodes Town: €13.

C

CAMPING

There are no longer any official campsites on Rhodes. Unofficial camping is forbidden – however, this doesn't seem to deter the hundreds of windsurfers who head down to Prasonísi in the summer in their motor-homes. With no facilities, this area can become full of litter by the end of the season.

CAR RENTAL

Rhodes is a good destination for exploration by car. Most of the roads are in good condition, and distances are generally very manageable. You won't need a vehicle for Rhodes Town itself, but having a car frees you from standard tour-group itineraries and allows you to visit sites at off-peak times of the day.

Booking before you arrive through a major international car-rental company will guarantee your vehicle, as in peak season demand will be high. Hertz, Avis and Europcar all have franchise offices at the airport, but these are only open during regular office hours and if you intend to pick up a car after 9pm you may need to pay a surcharge. All the major hotels down to C grade will be able to arrange car rental where the car will be delivered to the hotel.

Hertz (Rhodes airport office): Tel. 2241 036 702;
website <www.hertz.com>.
Avis (Rhodes airport office): Tel. 2241 082 896;
website <www.avis.com>.
Europcar (Rhodes airport office): Tel. 2241 083 105;
website <www.europcar.com>.

You don't have to rely on the major international names. There are many reputable local rental agencies that give reasonable service should you decide to rent once you reach the islands. You may also find that local companies can be more flexible than international ones with pricing, especially in low season. Their cars are generally in good condition. One company with several offices on the island is Galaxy Car Rental, Tel. 2241 033 135.

Those who want to rent should carry an international licence, although a national licence is usually accepted provided that it has been held for one full year and the driver is over 21 years of age. Deposits are usually waived for those paying by credit card.

Insurance. Insurance is often included in the rental rates but do ask about this and read the contract thoroughly to be sure. Collision damage waiver is advisable; if your credit card or home insurance does not provide such as waiver, it should be purchased as part of the rental agreement.

Moped/scooter/motorcycle rental. Renting a small motorbike is one of the most popular ways of cruising the resorts. Rental is relatively inexpensive – around €20 per day for a 50cc machine, lower if you hire it for three days or more. However, there are a number of dangers in moped rental, not least the safety factor – every year there are a number of serious injuries and fatalities involving riders. The government has passed legislation making it illegal to rent any motorised bike over 50cc without a motorcycle licence. Many rental agencies have not passed on this information to renters. If you hire a motorcycle over 50cc without a motorcycle licence, any insurance you have will be void and could create grave difficulties if you are injured or involved in an accident.

Those who rent scooters or mopeds should wear helmets (this is the law in Greece, although rarely enforced) and proceed with caution, especially on corners where ground dust and gravel make the road surface slippery.

CLIMATE

It is said that Rhodes benefits from 300 sunny days each year. Certainly from April until the end of October you can almost be guaranteed blue skies. Temperatures reach a sweltering 38°C (100 °F) in the summer months with hot nights, although the nights become cooler early and late in the season.

The Meltemi wind that blows down from the Caucasus through the Aegean meets the northwest coast of the island, making the west coast a little cooler throughout the year. The east coast has fewer breezes, and Líndos can be very oppressive on a hot, still summer afternoon.

There is some rain in winter, and the air feels damp at that time of year, although the temperature is rarely particularly cold.

Temperature

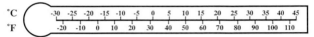

CLOTHING

In summer you require very little clothing on Rhodes. For daytime on the beach, you'll need swimwear and a pair of plastic beach sandals (for pebbly beaches), plus a layer to cover up and stop sunburn. For sightseeing, dress in shorts or lightweight trousers and T-shirts, or lightweight dresses. Remember to bring comfortable shoes for archaeological sites. Natural fibres will help to absorb perspiration and allow the skin to breathe. Cotton and silk clothing is ideal. If you intend to visit churches or monasteries, appropriate dress is compulsory. Both sexes should cover their shoulders. Men should wear lightweight trousers, and women should wear a skirt that covers the knees.

Don't forget a hat and good sunglasses, as the strong sun creates a lot of glare, which can tire eyes very quickly.

For evenings, very few places have any dress code, although in smarter hotels men are required to wear long trousers.

A light sweater is useful for chilly evenings, especially in early or late season, as both spring and autumn can be cool after the sun has dropped. It can also get remarkably chilly after dark on the decks of ferries, so if you take a day excursion and intend to return late, a cotton sweater or fleece might be a good idea.

COMPLAINTS

If you have a complaint it's best to raise it first with the owner of the establishment concerned. If you are not satisfied, take your complaint to the tourist police (see CRIME AND SAFETY), there will be a number of officers on the island who deal solely with the complaints from, and with the safety of, visitors. They will speak English.

CRIME AND SAFETY

Despite atrocious behaviour in summer 2003 by British holiday-makers in Faliráki, Rhodes is generally relatively safe both in terms of personal safety and the safety of your belongings. Most visitor problems tend to centre around motorbike accidents and over-indulgence in sun or alcohol. Serious crime is rare, but it is still important to guard against becoming a victim. Lock any valuables in the hotel safe. Don't leave valuables unsupervised on the beach or on view in your rental car.

As a matter of personal safety, don't get into a car with a stranger and always use official taxis, especially if you are travelling alone.

If you find yourself a victim of crime contact the Tourist Police, Tel. 2241 027 423. These officers will speak English.

CUSTOMS AND ENTRY REQUIREMENTS

EU citizens can visit Greece and the islands for an unlimited amount of time. Irish citizens need some proof of identity, and British citizens must have a valid passport. Citizens of the US, Canada, Australia and New Zealand can stay for up to three months with a valid passport. South African citizens can stay for up to two months with a valid passport. No visas are needed for these stays. If you wish to extend these time-scales you must obtain a permit from the Aliens Bureau, 173 Alexandras Avenue, 11 522 Athens. Tel. 2107 705 701.

Greece has some strict regulations about the import of drugs. All the obvious ones are illegal (as well as some other drugs such as codeine or tranquillisers), and there are strict laws with strong punitive measures for anyone breaking the rules. If you take any drug on the advice of your doctor always carry enough for your needs in an official container – medicines for personal use are permitted.

The Greek authorities are very concerned about the loss of antiquities and national treasures. If you intend to buy an old piece, always deal with a reputable dealer and keep your receipts. Genuine antiques will require a permit. Exporting antiques without a permit is considered a serious offense.

Since the abolishment of duty-free allowances for all EU countries, all goods brought into Greece from Britain and Ireland must be duty-paid. In theory there are no limitations to the amount of duty-paid goods that can be brought into the country. However, be aware that cigarettes and most spirits are relatively inexpensive in Greece.

For citizens of non-EU countries, allowances for goods bought duty-free to be carried into Greece (and Rhodes) are as follows:

200 cigarettes or 50 cigars or 250 grammes of tobacco.
1 litre of spirits or 4 litres of wine.
250 ml of cologne or 50 ml of perfume.

 D

DRIVING
Road conditions. Road conditions have improved greatly in the last few years, and there are few parts of the island not accessible to a normal rental car. However, the roads have no shoulders, only dust and stones along the sides. This can cause problems, especially for bike riders who need to drive towards the centre of the road to avoid the loose surface. If you get caught in a summer storm, the road surface can become very slippery.

Rhodes

Rules and regulations. In Greece, you should drive on the right and pass on the left, yielding to vehicles from the right. The majority of road signs are international and easy to understand. Since many place names in Roman lettering are written phonetically, you may find the same village name is written several different ways as you drive along.

Speed limits on open roads are 100 kmh (65mph) and in towns 50 kph (30 mph) unless otherwise stated, although many local people do not adhere to the regulations. Both speed limit and distance signs are in kilometres.

Seat belts are compulsory, as are crash helmets when riding a motorcycle. Drunk-driving laws are strict, and police can issue on-the-spot fines.

Many island towns have one-way systems to ease the flow of traffic around the narrow streets. Be aware that many moped riders (and some car drivers) do not obey these rules. Many are inexperienced and may not be properly insured. Give them plenty of room if possible.

Pedestrians also have their own agendas. They will often walk in the roadway, and step out without looking as they are in laid-back holiday mode.

Fluid measures

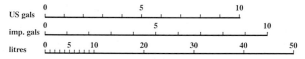

Distance

Petrol costs. Petrol is comparitively cheap by European standards at around €0.80 per litre of unleaded petrol and €0.68 per litre of diesel. Petrol stations have been growing in number in recent years but it is wise not to let your tank get too low, especially if you intend to explore the south of the island. Petrol stations are open every day in season, between the hours of 9am and 7pm.

If you need help: always carry the telephone number of your rental office with you when you travel, as someone there will be able to advise you if you have difficulties. In case of accident or theft, contact the Tourist Police who will send an English-speaking officer to help you.

Road signs. Most road signs are the standard pictographs used throughout Europe. However, you may also see some of these written signs:

No through road	ΑΔΙΕΞΟΔΟΣ
No entry	ΑΠΑΓΟΡΕΥΕΤΑΙ Η ΕΙΣΟΔΟΣ
No parking	ΑΠΑΓΟΡΕΥΕΤΑΙ Η
Roadworks in progress	ΕΡΓΑ ΕΠΙ ΤΗΣ ΟΔΟΥ
Caution	ΚΙΝΔΥΝΟΣ
One-way traffic	ΜΟΝΟΔΡΟΜΟΣ
Bus stop	ΣΤΑΣΙΣ

Are we on the right road for…?	**Ímaste sto sostó drómo giá…?**
Full tank, please.	**Na to gemísete parakaló.**
normal/super/lead-free/diesel	**aplí/soúper/amólivdos/petréleo**
Check the oil/tires/battery.	**Na elénxete ta ládia/ta lásticha/ti bataría.**
My car has broken down.	**Épatha mía vlávi.**
There's been an accident.	**Égine éna atíchima.**

E

ELECTRICITY

The electric current is 220 volts/50 cycles. Electric plugs are of the European continental two-/three-prong type. Adaptor plugs are available in the main islands but it is best to buy one at home before you leave.

an adaptor   **énas metaschimatistís**

EMBASSIES AND CONSULATES

All national embassies are located in Athens, the capital of Greece.

Australian Embassy and Consulate. 37 D. Soutsou Street, 115 21 Athens. Tel. 2106 450 404; fax 2106 466 595.

British Embassy and Consulate. 1 Ploutarchou Street, 106 75 Athens. Tel. 2107 236 211; fax 2107 241 872, 2107 230 954

There is a *British Consulate* on the island. Pavlou Mela 3, Rhodes New Town, 85100 Rhodes. Tel. 2241 027 247

Canadian Embassy. 4 Gennadiou Street, 115–21 Athens. Tel. 2107 273 400; fax 2107 273 460

Irish Embassy. 7, Vass. Konstantinou Avenue, 106 74 Athens. Tel. 2107 232 771/2; fax 2107 240 217

New Zealand General Consulate. 24 Xanias Street, 115 28 Athens. Tel. 2106 874 700; fax 2106 874 444

South African Embassy and Consulate. 60 Kifisias Avenue, 151 25 Marousi. Tel. 2106 806 645; fax 2106 806 640

US Embassy and Consulate. 91 Vas. Sofias Avenue, 115 27 Athens. Tel. 2107 212 951; fax 2106 456 282

EMERGENCIES

The following emergency numbers are used on the island.

Police 100	Ambulance 166
Tourist Police 2241 027 423	Fire 199
Traffic Police 2241 022 346	Forestry Fire Service 191

G

GAY AND LESBIAN TRAVELLERS

Greece is traditionally a very conservative country where traditional family relationships form the backbone of society. However, there is a natural courtesy towards visitors and this, combined with the number of different types of international tourists, makes Rhodes a good destination for gay and lesbian travellers.

GETTING THERE

By Air. Olympic Airways is the national carrier of Greece. It offers scheduled flights to Rhodes Paradísi Airport at least four times per day from its hub, Athens airport. These link with Olympic Airlines and other international carrier flights into Athens but can be filled quickly in summer and must be booked well in advance. Olympic Airways website <www.olympic-airways.gr>.

Olympic Airways operates international flights to Athens from the following destinations: New York, Toronto, London and Manchester. It operates to and from the following European cities for flight connections from the UK, US, Australia, New Zealand and South Africa: Amsterdam, Brussels, Frankfurt, Geneva, Zurich, Milan, Rome and Paris.

Numerous international carriers fly into Athens. These include Lufthansa (<www.lufthansa.com>), KLM (website <www.klm.com>), Swiss (website <www.swiss.com>) and British Airways (website <www.britishairways.com>). Connections from the US to Europe can be achieved with American Airlines (website <www.aa.com>), Delta Airlines (website <www.delta.com>), Continental Airlines (website <www.continental.com>), Virgin Airlines (website <www.virgin-atlantic.com>). From Australia and New Zealand you can reach Europe for onward flights to Greece with Singapore Airlines (website <www.singaporeair.com>), Thai Airways (website <www.thaiair.com>), Qantas (website <www.qantas.com>) and Air New Zealand (website <www.airnewzealand.co.nz>).

Rhodes

Many visitors to Rhodes arrive on charter aircraft. British companies such as Virgin Holidays (website <www.virginholidays.com>), Thomson (website <www.thomsonholidays.com>), Airtours (website <www.airtours.com>), Manos (website <www.manos.co.uk>) and Direct Greece (website <www.directholidays.co.uk>) offer flight only and package deals from airports in the UK, in addition to German, French, Italian and Swiss companies flying from around Europe.

By Boat. Rhodes is connected to Piraeus, the port for Athens, by daily car and passenger ferry. Sailings fall in number after the end of September, increasing after April. Boats can be very busy at peak times, and it is advisable to buy a ticket as far in advance as possible. Commercial ticket agents in Athens or Piraeus will be able to advise you on sailings and prices. The company operating the majority of the sailings is Dane Sea Lines. Head Office: 92 Odós Australias; Tel. 2241 077 078; fax 2241077 084. Travelling time is 20–25 hours.

There are also daily sailings, linking Rhodes with Turkey.

GUIDES AND TOURS

Rhodes has several companies offering a range of well-organised tours with guides to the major sites and attractions. These will be offered at a price premium compared with organising them yourself, but you may feel that it is worth the extra for the convenience of being transported by coach. In Rhodes Town, Triton Holidays offer tours, travel tickets and much more. They are located at 25 Odós Plastíra; Tel. 2241 021 690; fax 2241 031 625; <www.tritondmc.gr>.

HEALTH AND MEDICAL CARE.

Emergency treatment is given free but this covers only immediate treatment. EU residents will be able to get further free treatment but must carry form E111 to obtain it. E111 forms must be validated before you leave home.

It is always advisable to take out health/accident insurance to cover you for a health emergency while on a trip. Insurance will reimburse the cost of protracted treatment or repatriation should the need arise.

There are no vaccination requirements for your trip.

As mentioned in the Customs section above, many medicines and prescription drugs obtained normally in other countries are banned in Greece. If you are taking any medication, take enough for your needs while on your trip and always keep it in its original packaging with original labels in case the customs agents have a query about it.

If you have a basic medical need, look for a pharmacy, or *farmakió*, signified by a green cross, where you will be able to obtain advice. Most pharmacists will speak some English.

Rhodes does have scorpions and snakes, although not in great numbers, and they tend to only be found off the beaten track. When exploring archaeological sites it is always wise to watch your footing and make some noise to ensure the creatures have time to escape before you arrive. A more common nuisance is the mosquito, especially on a balmy night. Always carry and use mosquito repellent when walking in the undergrowth, and as the sun sets.

Spiny sea urchins cause a number of injuries each year for swimmers. Avoidance is the best option, so invest in plastic sandals to protect your feet while in the sea.

The sun is strong in Greece, especially as the summer breezes seem to cool the air, so it is important to use appropriate protection. Limit your time in the sun, apply sunblock regularly and always have a cover with you in case of over-exposure. Children's skin should always be well protected when they are out in the sunshine.

Go easy on alcohol, which can cause dehydration. Although the tap water is safe to drink, bottled water often tastes better and is universally available. Always carry water with you to the beach or when sightseeing to protect against dehydration.

Rhodes' main hospital is situated in the New Town on Odós Erithrou Stavrou, Tel. 2241 080 000.

HITCHHIKING

Hitchhiking is not illegal in Greece and the islands, however public transport is comprehensive and inexpensive. Hitchhiking is a dangerous method of travel even in relatively safe destinations such as Rhodes. Women travelling alone are especially at risk.

HOLIDAYS

National Holidays fall on the following dates:

1 January: New Year's Day or Protochroniá.

6 January: Epiphany

25 March: Greek Independence Day.

1 May: May Day.

15 August: Assumption of the Virgin.

28 October: National 'No' or 'Ochi' Day.

25 December: Christmas Day.

26 December: St Stephen's Day.

Moveable dates centre around the Easter celebrations with the first day of Lent (Clean Monday), Good Friday, Easter Monday, the Ascension and Holy Monday (Whit Monday).

LANGUAGE

There is one uniform Greek language spoken by the whole populace, with minor dialectical variations. You will occasionally see signs written in the now-obsolete 'purist' *(katharévousa)* form, but the current 'popular' *(dhimotikí)* form is used by everyone.

The Greek alphabet consists of 24 letters, nine of which are the same as their Latin alphabet equivalent, five of which are similar to Latin alphabet letters and ten of which are uniquely Greek.

A	α	a	as in b**a**t
B	β	v	
Γ	γ	g	as in **g**o but softer (pronounced 'y' before 'e' and 'i')
Δ	δ	d	like **th** in **th**is
E	ε	e	as in g**e**t
Z	ζ	z	as in ja**zz**
H	η	i	like **ee** in meet
Θ	θ	th	as in **th**in
I	ι	i	like **i** in this
K	κ	k	
Λ	λ	l	
M	μ	m	
N	ν	n	
Ξ	ξ	x	like **ks** in than**k**s
O	ο	o	as in h**o**t
Π	π	p	
P	ρ	r	
Σ	σ/ς	s	as in ki**ss**
T	τ	t	
Y	υ	i	like **ee** in meet
Φ	φ	f	
X	χ	ch	as in Scottish lo**ch**
Ψ	ψ	ps	as in ti**ps**y
Ω	ω	o	as in b**o**ne

Numbers

1	**éna**	2	**dío**	3	**tría**
4	**téssera**	5	**pénde**	6	**éxi**

Rhodes

7	eftá	8	októ	9	enniá
10	déka	100	ekató	1,000	chília

Days of the Week

Sunday	**Kyriakí**	Thursday	**Pémpti**
Monday	**Deftéra**	Friday	**Paraskeví**
Tuesday	**Tríti**	Saturday	**Sávvato**
Wednesday	**Tetárti**		

Months

January	**Ianouários**	July	**Ioúlios**
February	**Fevrouários**	August	**Ávgoustos**
March	**Mártios**	September	**Septémvrios**
April	**Aprílios**	October	**Októvrios**
May	**Máïos**	November	**Noémvrios**
June	**Ioúnios**	December	**Dekémvrios**

Don't worry if you don't speak any Greek. You will find that most people working within the tourist industry will have a basic English vocabulary, and many speak English very well. You will also find that the *Berlitz Greek Phrase Book and Dictionary* covers nearly all the situations you're likely to encounter in your travels.

LAUNDRY AND DRY CLEANING

Express Laundry on Odós Kostí Palamá near the New Market (Tel. 2241 022 514) is open Monday–Saturday 8am–10pm and you can leave your laundry while you take in the sights.

When will it be ready?	**Póte tha íne étimo?**
I must have this for tomorrow morning.	**Prépi na íne étimo ávrio to proí.**

MAPS

You'll find a range of free maps at hotels, car-rental offices, all with advertising. These are adequate for exploring the attractions of the Old Town though not precise enough to pinpoint shops and restaurants on smaller side streets. Most maps of Rhodes and other Greek Islands are out-of-date because of rapid improvements in road conditions. The Road Edition 'Rhodes' map is one of the best commercial maps available.

MEDIA

Press. You'll be able to buy all the major European newspapers, including the Paris-produced *International Herald Tribune*, on the island although they will be one day old. *Athens News* is an English-language newspaper produced in Athens and available all across Greece. For local news and tourist information, a range of free multilingual magazines are filled with information for visitors and are published monthly. The English-language version is called the *Rodos News*.

TV. Most of the 'de Luxe' and A-class hotels have a range of satellite channels including CNN and BBC World.

MONEY

Currency. The euro (€) is the official currency used in Greece. Notes are denominated in 5, 10, 20, 50, 100, 200 and 500 euros; coins in 1 and 2 euros and 1, 2, 5, 10, 20 and 50 cents.

Currency Exchange. Most banks will offer currency exchange for foreign currency and travellers cheques and will charge a percentage commission for the service. This varies but is usually between 1% and 3%. Exchange rates should be published on a notice board inside the bank or in the window and are generally the same for each bank.

You can also exchange money and travellers cheques at commercial exchange centres found in all the main tourist destinations.

Rhodes

These are often open longer hours than the banks. Some of these advertise commission-free transactions, but exchange rates vary so you will need to decide which gives the better deal.

You will always need to prove your identity when exchanging money, so take your passport with you.

Automatic Teller Machines (ATMs). There are ATMs in the major resort areas in Rhodes Town, Líndos, Ixiá, and Faliráki, and at least one in the larger settlements inland. These usually accept both major credit and debit cards, and are the easiest (and cheapest) way of obtaining euros. Long queues can develop when the island becomes busy, and machines can be either empty or out-of-order, so it is sensible not to rely on ATMs as your sole form of obtaining cash.

Electric Currency Exchange. Next to an ATM you may also find a currency exchange machine that will accept notes of all major currencies outside the euro zone and deliver you euros in exchange. Just follow the instructions.

Credit Cards. Many hotels, restaurants, ticket offices and shops accept credit cards, but there is still a sizeable minority that do not. Some may charge extra for credit card payments, to cover their extra costs. It is always advisable to ask about credit card acceptance before you sign the register or order your food, to avoid difficulties later. It may also help to carry cash to cover meals, rather than rely on your credit card, perhaps €25–35 per person/per day.

Travellers cheques. These can be used to obtain cash at banks and hotels but are not generally accepted as payment in shops and restaurants. You will need a form of identification, such as a passport, to cash travellers cheques.

Can I pay with this credit card? | **Boró na pliróso me aftí ti pistotikí kárta?**

Do you accept travellers cheques? | **Pérnete travellers cheques?**

OPENING HOURS

Opening hours can be a little complicated and vary between official organisations, and privately owned shops and cafes. They also vary greatly between high and low season. Always be aware that the siesta is an important part of the day, and most establishments will be closed in the afternoons. It is best to visit any establishment in the mornings.

Banks are open Mon–Thurs 8am–2pm, Fri 8am–1.30pm.

Most museums are open Mon–Fri 8am–2pm and 5pm–7pm (this will vary). Most archaeological sites are open throughout the day and are closed on Mondays in winter.

Shops are open Mon–Sat 8am–2pm and 5pm–8.30pm although in peak season they may stay open until midnight, especially when selling tourist-related products.

The main post office is open Mon–Fri 8am–8pm.

Restaurants and tavernas begin dinner service at around 6pm, but most Greek families don't eat until after 9pm – this is when you get the best local atmosphere.

POLICE

Ordinary police wear a green uniform. They deal with traffic offenses and may impose fines for speeding and vehicle checks. The Tourist Police is a branch of the force that deals with tourist problems and complaints. They speak English and wear a dark grey uniform.

Police patrols take place regularly in Ixía, Faliráki and Rhodes New Town. On the rest of the island, patrols are almost non-existent, however crime is also rare so it is unlikely that you will need their services.

Emergency and traffic – 100.   Non-emergency – 0241 23849.
Tourist police – 2241 027 423. Traffic police – 2241 022 346.

Rhodes

| Where's the nearest police station? | **Pou íne to kodinótero astinomikió tmíma?** |

POST OFFICES

Post offices (painted bright yellow and blue with the initials ELTA) are generally open from 7.30am–2pm. Stamps can be bought here and at kiosks and tobacconists/newsagents for a small premium. Post offices also handle currency exchange, cash cheques and deal with money orders.

The price for sending a postcard to other EU countries is €0.52, further afield €0.73.

A stamp for this letter/ postcard, please.	**Ena grammatosimo giafto to gramma/kart postal, parakalo.**
I want to send a telegramme to …	**Thélo na stílo éna tilegráfima sto…**
Have you received any mail for... ?	**Échete grámmata giá …?**

PUBLIC TRANSPORT

Bus. The bus network links all the major settlements on the island with Rhodes Town and operates from early morning until around 9pm. For longer journeys, such as Rhodes to Líndos, services run hourly with the last service leaving Rhodes at 7.30pm. Services to Faliráki depart every 30 minutes until 9pm. Buses for the east side of the island depart from Odós Papágou. At the site of the Sound and Light Show venue, you'll find a kiosk that will issue photocopied timetables. For the west side and the airport, buses depart from Odós Avérof street on the north side of the New Market. There is a kiosk with timetables located here as well.

Taxis. The island is well equipped with taxis – mostly comfortable Mercedes sedans. Prices are fixed and posted from the airport and from Rhodes Town (Rimini Square) to various towns and attractions around the island. If your hotel calls a taxi for you, the receptionist will give you the taxi number. Most taxi drivers are honest but it pays to have a general idea of the fare before you depart. Be aware that some extra long or short journeys are unpopular with drivers who may refuse to take you. It is quite common to share your taxi with others travelling in the same direction.

Ferries. There are regular commercial ferry services from Rhodes to Chálki, Symi, Kálymnos, Kos, Leros, Nisyros, Patmos Samos, and Tilos, as well as connections to Piraeus and Thessaloníki on the Greek mainland. The main passenger port is next to Mandraki harbour, and numerous ticket agents can arrange your passage.

What's the fare to…?   **Piá íne í timí giá…?**

Could you give me a receipt?   **Miá apódhixi parákalo?**

RELIGION
Most of the population belongs to the Greek Orthodox Church. There is a Roman Catholic Church and a synagogue in Rhodes Town – details of services available from the Municipal Tourist Office (see below).

TELEPHONES
The international code for Greece is 30. All telephone numbers in Rhodes have 10 digits. Numbers in the north begin with 2241, while those in the south start with 2244.

There are many card-operated telephone booths across the island. You can make international calls from these. Cards can be bought at tourist offices, OTE offices, tobacconists/newsagents, and from some hotels. Use these for both domestic and direct-dial international calls. Directions will appear in English on most machines.

Rhodes

Most better-class hotels will have direct-dial facilities but will charge a high premium for calls.

International country codes are as follows, all prefixed by 00.

Australia 61	Germany 49	United Kingdom 44
Canada 1	Ireland 353	United States 1
France 33	New Zealand 64	South Africa 27

TIME ZONES

Greece operates two hours ahead of Greenwich Mean Time and also operates Daylight Savings Time – moving the clocks one hour forward during the summer.

If it is noon in Athens in August, here is the time in some other cities around the world.

London	New York	Jo'burg	**Athens**	Sydney	Auckland
10am	5am	11am	**12pm**	7pm	9pm

TIPPING

Service is included in restaurant and bar bills, although it is customary to leave any small change on the table. If you have a young boy or girl bring you water or clear your table it is customary to give them a few coins.

Taxi drivers expect a 10% tip.

Hotel chambermaids should be left a tip of around €1 per day. Bellhops and doormen should be tipped up to €2, depending on services provided.

Attendants in toilets should be left around €0.30.

TOILETS

There are a number of free public toilets in Rhodes Old Town. You'll find them in the New Market, near the bus and taxi station, and on the street behind the Suleiman Mosque. In Líndos you'll find them in the small town square bus station. Most museums also have good facilities.

TOURIST INFORMATION

The South Aegean Region Tourism Directorate for the Dodecanese, tel. 2241 935 226, website <www.ando.gr/eot>, open Mon–Fri 8am–3pm, formerly the GNTO, is responsible for producing and dispersing tourist information. The organisation has a network of offices throughout the world but official representation in the islands is very scarce, leaving the market open to lots of unofficial information bureaux, which vary greatly in quality. For tourist information before you travel to Greece, contact one of the following offices:

Australia and New Zealand

Greek National Tourist Organization, 51–75 Pitt Street, Sydney. New South Wales. Postal Address is PO Box R203 Royal Exchange, New South Wales 2000, Australia. Tel. (2) 92411663-5; fax 92352174.

Canada

Greek National Tourist Organization. 1300 Bay Street, Main Level, Toronto, Ontario M5R 3K8. Tel. (416) 968 2220; fax (416) 9686533; e-mail <gnto.tor@sympatico.ca>.

There is also an information office at 1170 place du Frère André, Suite 300, Montreal, Quebec H3B 3C6. Tel. (514) 8711535; fax (514) 8711498.

UK and Ireland

Greek National Tourist Organization. 4, Conduit Street, London W1R 0DJ. Tel. (020) 7734 5997; fax (020) 7287 1369; e-mail <eot-greektouristoffice@btinternet.com>.

US

Greek National Tourism Organization. Olympic Tower, 645 Fifth Avenue, New York, NY 10022. Tel. (212) 421 5777; fax (212) 826 6940; e-mail <gnto@greektourism.com>.

Rhodes

There is also a Rhodes Town Municipal Tourist Office on Rimini Square (near the main taxi stand) Tel. 2241 035 945. Open May–October Monday–Friday 8am–7pm, Saturday 8am–6pm. Copies of *Rodos News* are stocked here.

WEBSITES

There are a number of useful websites to help you plan your visit to Rhodes. Among the most informative are <www.rodos.com>, which is owned and operated by the Greek Travel Network; and <www.helios.gr>, which offers on-line booking, maps, and a calendar of upcoming events.

WEIGHTS AND MEASURES

Rhodes (and the rest of Greece) use the metric system. For length, weight and temperature conversions, see below.

Length

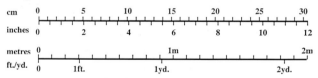

Weight

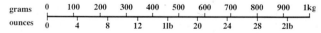

Temperature

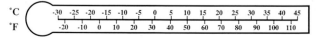

Recommended Hotels

Rhodes has a good range of accommodation, but because it is such a popular holiday island, many hotels have contracts with the major European travel-package companies, limiting the number of rooms available to independent travellers. Accommodation can be difficult to find in peak season - mid-July until the beginning of September. Always have a confirmed reservation if you travel at this time.

Prices also vary by as much as 40 percent between high and low season. Most hotels have several different types of room, including suites and bungalows, so be sure to confirm the type of accommodation that you are booking. Some open all year, while the majority are open from April to November only.

Hotels are graded and approved by the Greek Tourist Organisation (EOT) according to facilities offered rather than quality and comfort. A good B- or C-grade hotel might therefore offer more than an A-grade one.

Rooms are also available in private houses – some are approved and graded by the EOT; these can offer a more authentic Greek experience. Although the prices below refer to rates at peak time for a double room, the differential in prices should remain constant between hotels throughout the year. Most hotels take credit cards unless noted below.

If you are telephoning from outside Greece, use the country code 30, followed by the hotel's own telephone or fax number.

€	45 euros and under
€€	45–75 euros
€€€	75–100 euros
€€€€	100–130 euros
€€€€	over 130 euros

RHODES TOWN

Cava d'Oro Hotel €€€ *Kistinioú 15, 851 00 Rhodes; tel: 2241 036 980*. In the eastern part of the Old Town, this small hotel hit

Rhodes

the headlines when British broadcaster Michael Palin stayed here on his Pole to Pole expedition. Located off the main tourist routes, this hotel is relatively quiet.

The Esperia Hotel €€ *Gríva 7, 851 00 Rhodes; tel: 2241 023 941; fax: 2241 077501.* The refurbished Esperia is a good budget option, close to the lively northern New Town. Offers better accommodation than its price suggests.

Hotel Anastasia €€ *28th Oktovríou 46, 851 00 Rhodes; tel: 2241 028 007; fax: 2241 021 815; <www.anastasia-hotel.com>.* Set in a pleasant garden with banana trees and resident tortoises, the Anastasia is an oasis in a predominantly cement jungle. One of the few old-fashioned hotels left in the New Town. Cash only.

Hotel Mediterranean €€€€ *Kos 35, 851 00 Rhodes; tel: 2241 024 661; fax: 2241 022 828; <www.mediterranean.gr>.* Within walking distance of the Old Town and set on the New Town's sandy beach, the Mediterranean is a renovated art deco hotel. Facilities include room service, a restaurant, cafe and freshwater pool.

Hotel Spot € *Perikléous 21, 851 00 Rhodes; tel: 2241 034 737; fax: 2241 034 737; <www.rodosisland.gr>.* A well cared-for budget option, Hotel Spot stands out above others in its range. All the rooms have a homely feel, and the English-speaking owner is a welcoming host. Cash only.

Ibiscus €€€ *Nisýrou 17, 851 00 Rhodes; tel: 2241 024 421; fax: 2241 027 283; <e-mail: ibiscus@rhotel.gr>.* Renovated in 2002, this pleasant New Town hotel combines the best of both a business and holiday environment with its leather lounges and marble floors. Apartment-style rooms are available.

Mansion Marco Polo €€€ *Agíou Fanouríou 42, 851 00 Rhodes; tel: 2241 025 562; fax: 2241 025 562; <www. marcolopolomansion.web.com>*. Hardly noticeable off a cobbled alleyway, this discrete guesthouse is stunning at first sight. A restored Ottoman *caravanserai*, it combines old-world charm with modern-day comfort. With an excellent restaurant and cafe, Marco Polo is one of the classiest places to stay in Rhodes.

Niki's Rooms € *Sofokléous 39, 851 00 Rhodes; tel: 2241 025 115*. Set in the south central Old Town, Niki's is a good budget option for sightseers. Each room has its own bathroom – those rooms on the upper floor have balconies. Communal terrace, washing machine and shared fridge. Cash only.

Pension Andreas €€€ *Omírou 28d, 851 00 Rhodes; tel: 2241 034 156; fax: 2241 074 285; <www.hotelandreas.com>*. In the quietest part of the Old Town is this exquisite little pension with rather small but comfortable rooms. The staff's attentive care and welcoming smiles mean that guests often come for one night and stay for a week or more.

Rodos Park Suites Hotel €€€€ *Ríga Feréou 12, 851 00 Rhodes; tel: 2241 024 612; fax: 2241 024 613; <www.greekhotel. com>*. Close to the city walls, the Rodos Park is a perfect for exploring the old city. Facilities include a restaurant, bars, pool and health club.

AROUND THE ISLAND

Atrium Palace Resort Hotel €€€€€ *Kálathos Beach, 851 02 Rhodes; tel: 2244 031 601; fax: 2244 031 600; <www.atri-um.gr.>*. The large Atrium Palace sits on a wide sandy bay, 6 km (4 miles) from Líndos on the east coast, and is attractively set around a pool area and gardens. Facilities include a restaurant, bar, room service, indoor and outdoor pools, tennis and basket-ball courts, shops, hairdresser, free gym and sauna, and a children's club.

Daniel Hotel € *Kálathos, 851 02 Rhodes; tel: 2244 031 584; fax: 2244 031 583; <www.danielhotel.gr>*. On the main street in Kálathos, around five minute's walk from the beach, is a small, modern hotel. There is a modest pool and terrace at the rear with a bar.

Esperos Palace €€€ *Faliráki, 851 00 Rhodes; tel: 2241 086 046; fax: 2241 085 741; <www.esperia-hotels.gr>*. This large hotel complex, located right on the sandy beach, offers guests a mix of resort activities and the Faliráki nightlife. The impressive range of facilities includes two restaurants, six bars, outdoor and indoor pools with water rides, room service, a gym, shops and tennis courts.

Kresten Palace Hotel €€€ *Kallithéa, 851 00 Rhodes; tel: 2241 062 714; fax: 2241 065 976; <www.helios.gr>*. Located 6 km (4 miles) south of Rhodes Town on bus route, this hotel sits on a rocky bay with a small sandy beach and is wrapped in gardens and palm trees. Facilities include a restaurant, bar, large freshwater pool, children's club and pool, shop, tennis courts, gym and sauna.

Líndos Mare Hotel €€€€€ *Vlícha, 851 07 Rhodes; tel: 2244 031 130; fax: 2244 031 131; <www.lindosmare.gr>*. Situated on a hillside just 2 km (1.2 miles) north of Líndos, this hotel has a relaxed, friendly atmosphere. Rooms have air-conditioning, telephone, refridgerator, satellite television, and balcony or terrace. Facilities include a pool, children's play area, shops and no-smoking restaurant.

Miramare Wonderland €€€€€ *Ixiá, 851 00 Rhodes; tel: 2241 096 251; fax: 2241 095 954; <www.mamhotel.gr>.* Beautifully designed suites and bungalow hotel set in lush gardens by the beach in Ixiá, 3.5 km (2 miles) from Rhodes Old Town. Facilities include pools for both children and adults, shop, two restaurants, three bars, fitness room, watersports centre, children's club, shop, room service. A replica 19th-century train carries guests around the site.

Rodos Palace €€€€€ *Trianton Avenue, Ixiá, 85 100 Rhodes; tel: 2241 025222; fax 2241 025350; <www.rodos-palace. com>.* One of the oldest hotels in Rhodes, the Rodos Palace caters for all tastes, with a main wing, executive wing and bungalows set among 12 hectares (30 acres) of grounds. Extensive facilities include seven restaurants, three bars, a club, four pools, tennis courts, watersports, a fitness centre, sauna, shops and a children's club.

Rodos Palladium €€€€€ *On the beach, Faliráki, 851 00 Rhodes; tel: 2241 086 004; fax: 2241 086 424; <www.rodospalladium.gr>.* Built next to a wide sandy bay, 2 km (1.2 miles) to the north of Faliráki, the resort-style Palladium is one of the island's newest hotels. Facilities include two restaurants, bars, outdoor and indoor pools, a fitness centre, tennis courts and room service.

Rodos Princess €€€ *Asklipió, Kiotári, 851 09 Rhodes; tel: 2244 047 102; fax: 2244 047 267; <www.helioshotels.gr>.* For those who want to get away from it all, the Rodos Princess sits 18 km (11 miles) south of Líndos, well beyond the tourist traffic. The hotel is set in a garden that descends to a beach, and facilities include a restaurant, bar, fitness centre, outdoor and indoor pools and a children's club.

Rhodes

Sunrise Hotel €€ *Péfkos, 851 09 Rhodes; tel: 2244 048 311; fax: 2244 048 345.* The Sunrise is situated by a sandy beach, 5 km (3 miles) south of Líndos and south of Péfkos village, but close to local transport. Rooms have telephones, televisions, hairdryers and a balcony or terrace. Apartments with kitchenettes are also available. Facilities include a good-sized pool, restaurant, bar, tennis courts and shop.

SYMI

Hotel Aliki €€€ *Gialós, 856 00 Symi; tel: 2241 071 665; fax: 2241 071 665; <www.simi-hotelaliki.gr>.* This 1895 building on the coast road from the port of Gialós to Nos beach was tastefully converted into a boutique hotel in the 1990s. The Aliki offers well-furnished, simple accommodation with good views across to the harbour.

KOS

Hotel Afendoulis € *Evripílou 1, 853 00 Kos; tel: 2242 025 321; <e-mail: afendoulishotel@kos.forthnet.gr>.* The most pleasant, friendly place to stay in Kos is this cosy hotel run by an English-speaking family. The small but comfortable rooms all have fans. There is a pleasant ground-floor communal lobby and a patio area where guests can gather for drinks and gossip. Internet access is also available.

CHALKI

The Captain's House € *Emboriós, 851 10 Chalki; tel: 2246 045 201.* On an island where independent accommodation is hard to find, this 19th-century mansion with en-suite rooms is by far the best option. Sequestered in a quiet part of the village, this relaxing guesthouse enjoys a shaded garden and is run by English-speaking retired sea-captain Alex Sakellaridis and his wife Christine.

Recommended Restaurants

Restaurant and tavernas are plentiful on Rhodes and offer excellent value for money, although the range of food styles is limited compared with that in some cosmopolitan destinations. Owing to the number of European visitors, many restaurants offer English, Italian and French dishes on the menu, but the quality varies. A little effort to find authentic cuisine always pays dividends, so be on the lookout for small backstreet establishments frequented by local people.

Greek families eat out regularly, so restaurants are excellent places to make friends and find out a little about the local lifestyle. Just remember that Greeks will have had a siesta during the afternoon and don't set out to eat until 9pm at the earliest – if you want to soak in the authentic atmosphere, you'll need to ensure that your eating habits tie in with this.

The following recommendations range from authentic *ouzerís* and good-value tavernas to some of the most renowned restaurants on the island. Some places are a little difficult to find, having no formal address – if this is the case, ask at your hotel for directions.

Most restaurants open for lunch and dinner daily; when this is otherwise it is noted in the description. The majority of eateries do not take reservations, but where this is recommended, it is indicated in the description. Credit cards are not universally accepted, so double-check before you order.

€	10 euros and under
€€	10–15 euros
€€€	15–20 euros
€€€€	20–25 euros
€€€€€	over 25 euros

RHODES TOWN

Alexis €€€€ *Sokrátous 18, Old Town; tel: 2241 029 347.* One of the finest fish tavernas in the Greek islands, with a courtyard shaded by an old plane tree, Alexis has been open for 40 years. Fresh fish daily and organic vegetables grown by the family make for delicious *mezédhes* and *entrée* dishes. Open April–October. Major credit cards.

Begleri €€€ *Klavdíou Pépper 105–7, Zéfyros Beach; tel: 2241 033 353.* The Begleri stands out among the many mostly locals-only *ouzerí*-tavernas on the south side of the New Town. This eatery offers a wide range of fish dishes with excellent sea-urchin salad and pan-cooked mussels in cheese. Open all year except Sunday evening. Cash only.

Dinoris €€€€ *Plateía Mousíou 14a, Old Town; tel: 2241 025 824.* Located in a small alley off Plateía Mousíou (Museum Square) in a beautiful 14th-century building that used to be the stables for a Knights of St John inn, Dinoris is the perfect place for an elegant seafood meal. Good wine list. Open all year for lunch and dinner. Major credit cards.

Fotis €€€ *Menekléous 8, Old Town; tel: 2241 027 359.* This unpretentious fish taverna provides high quality without the hype. The fresh grilled fish is succulent and the cuttlefish in ink is also a good choice. Open all year. Major credit cards.

Fotis Melathron €€€€ *Párodos Sokrátous 41, Old Town; tel: 2241 023 272.* Tucked away out of sight of the main tourist restaurants in the Old Town, the Melathron has discreet dining areas decked out in stone and wood. The menu is traditional Greek cuisine – the large steaks are exceptional. One of the most impressive-looking restaurants on Rhodes. Open all year. Major credit cards.

Kasbah €€€ *Plátonos 4-8, Old Town; tel: 2241 078 633.* This primarily Moroccan restaurant with a few French-Greek overtones for good measure is unusual for Rhodes. Couscous features predominantly, and there are good vegetarian options. The wine list features Californian, Chilean and local wines, and dinner is accompanied by mood-enhancing world music. Open April–November. Major credit cards.

Maria's Taverna €€ *105-6 New Market, New Town; tel: 2241 020 853.* Of all the good-budget eateries in the New Market, Maria's takes a little more care than most with its decor and menu. Excellent slow-cooked meat dishes are equalled by the salads and *mezé* dishes, and all of this is backed up with good country house wine. Open April–October. Cash only.

Myrovolos €€€ *Láhitos 13, Old Town; tel: 2241 038 693.* Around the corner from Sokrátous you'll find this discrete hole in the wall where local diners gather. The dishes are predominantly *mezés*-based and include cuttlefish stuffed with feta. Live music is often played. There are only a few tables so arrive early for a good seat. Open May–October. Cash only.

Mystagogia €€ *Themistokléous 5, Old Town; tel: 241 032 981.* It can be hard to find this back-street taverna, but it's worth the effort. The atmospheric location on a narrow, cobbled street is complemented by the well-crafted traditional Greek dishes. Meaning 'initiation into mystic rights', Mystagogia will initiate you into some of the least fussy but still subtle, Greek cuisine around. Open all year. Cash only.

Nireas €€€€ *Sofokléous 22, Old Town; tel: 2241 021 703.* In a place with as many fish restaurants as Rhodes Town, finding a good one is a tall order, but Nireas is a good choice. The stone-clad, vine-covered building is tucked away almost out of sight, and you'll miss it if you blink. Apart from a wide range of fish there is a good selection of shellfish – clams, limpets, mussels

Rhodes

and the like – as well as the ever-popular tiny Symi prawns. Open all year. Cash only.

Palia Istoria €€€€ *Corner of Mitropóleos and Dendrinoú, New Town; tel: 2241 032 421.* This 1923 villa is one of the island's most popular restaurants and attracts mostly Greek customers. The menu features local and inspired international dishes. Good wine cellar for Greek labels. Open all year except Sundays; dinner only. Major credit cards.

Plaka Restaurant €€€ *Plateía Ippokrátous 3, Old Town; tel: 2241 035 695.* The terrace overlooking bustling Plateía Ippokrátous (Ippokrátous Square) is the main reason for eating at Plaka – the range of fish dishes and Italian cuisine is good, but it is the location that makes the restaurant really special. Open April–October. Major credit cards.

7.5 Thavmata (7.5 Wonders) €€€€ *Dilberáki 15, New Town; tel: 2241 038 905.* Housed in a 17th-century building, 7.5 Thavmata has created a following with its fusion cuisine, a mixture of Southeast Asian, Scandinavian and Mediterranean influences. Simple decor and a pretty garden add to the ambiance. Open March–October for dinner only. Major credit cards.

Synaxaria €€ *Aristofánous 47, New Town; tel: 2241 036 562.* Known locally as Maria's, after the owner, Synaxaria is a small eatery buried away in the back streets. This popular taverna does a great spin on traditional Rhodian dishes. Cuttlefish with spinach is one of the excellent items on the menu, as is the delicate lamb fricassée. Open May–October. Cash only.

Taverna Kostas €€ *Pythagóra 62, Old Town; tel: 2241 026 217.* Family-owned for over 30 years and situated on an old narrow street, Kostas is one of the most renowned local tavernas. Good taverna menu. Garden terrace. Open all year. Cash only.

AROUND THE ISLAND

Argo Restaurant €€€€€ *Haráki; tel: 2244 0051 410*. Haráki is renowned for its fish restaurants, and Argo is both the best and the most expensive. Set on a headland overlooking the bay, it has a pretty terrace for lunchtime or evening dining. Imaginative menu and a good wine list. Popular with the locals. Open all year. Major credit cards.

Arhondiko €€€€ *Líndos; tel: 2244 031 992*. The menu in this atmospheric early 17th-century captain's house is emphatically international Greek. While you can easily be distracted by the stone building's exquisite external and internal decor, the food is equally refined. The lobster in pasta, the leg of lamb stuffed with garlic, feta cheese, carrots and rosemary, and the stuffed vine leaves are all excellent. Open April–October. Major credit cards.

Bakis Taverna €€€ *Émbonas; tel: 2246 041 247*. This simple village square taverna serves excellent chargrilled meats with cuts from the family butcher shop, crisp salads and a range of other good Greek dishes. House wines from local grapes are served from the barrel. Open all year. Cash only.

Giannis Restaurant €€ *Koskinoú Village; tel: 2241 063 547*. Buried away on a narrow, paved back street in the village of Koskinoú, a short drive from Rhodes Town, Giannis is an unpretentious taverna. The succulent grills and *mezédhes* are top class, as are the suckling pig and Symi prawns. Open evenings only. Cash only.

Kalypso Restaurant €€€€ *Líndos; tel: 2244 031669*. Set in an historic captain's house, Kalypso offers Greek cuisine and also has a Middle Eastern influence in its dishes. You can eat on the terrace overlooking the rooftops of Líndos. Open April–October, closed Sundays. Major credit cards.

Rhodes

Martina's €€ *Kattaviá Village; tel: 2244 091 021.* Down in the deep south of Rhodes is the little village of Kattaviá , home to the small Greek-Italian taverna called Martina's. Reminiscent of a small grocer shop, Martina's serves up classic Greek and stock Italian pasta-based dishes. The spaghetti *puttanesca* is particularly rich and pungent. Open April–October. Cash only.

Masasoura €€ *Maritsá Village; tel: 2241 048 109.* Out in the central uplands, off the beaten track, is the little village of Maritsá. Sought out by Greeks for Sunday lunch, Masasoura is a simple, family-run grill-house and restaurant serving up locally produced meats, cheeses and vegetables. The potatoes are fabulous. Open all year; Sundays lunch only. Cash only.

Mavrikos €€€€ *Líndos; tel: 2244 031 232.* This family-run restaurant just off the main square is well regarded by locals and visitors alike for its exquisite oven-cooked dishes and fresh fish. Cuttlefish in rice, lobster in pasta, and rice with chickpeas are dishes that stand out in an extensive menu. Open April–November. Major credit cards.

Pigi Fasouli €€ *Psínthos; tel: 2241 056 259.* Located at the 7 Springs in the shade of the pine trees – you'll hear running water in the background – this is a good place for a snack or lunch after exploring the region. Expect ducks and geese for company as much as fellow tourists and locals. Open April–October 9am–7pm, November–March, weekends only. Cash only.

Ta Kioupia €€€€€ *Argonaftón 12, Ialysós; tel: 2241 093 448.* You'll need a large appetite to cope at this particular restaurant. If you order the set menu, you'll be served a seemingly endless string of gourmet delicacies and dishes, so pace yourself carefully or bring lots of friends to help you eat everything. There is also an extensive wine list. The walled garden, with candle-lit pool, has a lovely atmosphere. Open dinner only. Major credit cards.

SYMI

Estiatorio Mythos €€€ *Yialós; tel: 2246 071 488*. Set on the south side of the harbour this restaurant has two distinct menus. Pasta dominates at lunchtime, while in the evening the owner/chef turns out an array of imaginative *mezédhes*. Check the daily specials as well as the standard listings, which include good *saganaki* (skillet cooked) concoctions with cheese and mussels among other ingredients.

KOS

Petrus €€€€€ *Ippokrátous 3, Kos Town; tel: 2242 049 480*. Potentially the best, if not the classiest, bistro-style restaurant on Kos, Petrus combines choice Swiss-French flavours with select Greek ingredients to produce a superb mix of tastes and creations. The impressive salad selection makes for a meal in itself, and the roast partridge with fresh herby vegetables is particularly recommended. There almost 40 different wines stored in the cellars of the restaurant. Open for dinner only. Major credit cards.

CHALKI

Ftenagia Beach Taverna €€ *Emboriós; tel: 6945 998 333*. For such a small island, the culinary choices on Chálki are generally very good. While most its restaurants decorate the harbourside, a 15-minute walk will bring you to tiny Ftenagia Beach and its adjacent beach taverna. The service and food quality here are excellent, and the ambience at sunset is unmissable. Take an iced *oúzo* or two before dining on the day's specialities.

INDEX